Higher

Biology

2000 Exam
2001 Exam
2002 Exam
2002 Winter Diet Exam
2003 Exam

© Scottish Qualifications Authority
All rights reserved. Copying prohibited. No part of this publication may be reproduced, stored in a retrieval system, or transmitted in any form or by any means, electronic, mechanical, photocopying, recording or otherwise.
First exam published in 2000.
Published by
Leckie & Leckie, 8 Whitehill Terrace, St. Andrews, Scotland KY16 8RN
tel: 01334 475656 fax: 01334 477392
enquiries@leckieandleckie.co.uk www.leckieandleckie.co.uk
Leckie & Leckie Project Team: Peter Dennis; John MacPherson; Bruce Ryan; Andrea Smith
ISBN 1-84372-117-1
A CIP Catalogue record for this book is available from the British Library.
Printed in Scotland by Scotprint.
Leckie & Leckie is a division of Granada Learning Limited, part of Granada plc.

Leckie × Leckie
Scotland's leading educational publishers

Introduction

Dear Student,

This past paper book provides you with the perfect opportunity to put into practice everything you should know in order to excel in your exams. The compilation of papers will expose you to an extensive range of questions and will provide you with a clear idea of what to expect in your own exam this summer.

The past papers represent an integral part of your revision: the questions test not only your subject knowledge and understanding but also the examinable skills that you should have acquired and developed throughout your course. The answer booklet at the back of the book will allow you to monitor your ability, see exactly what an examiner looks for to award full marks and will also enable you to identify areas for more concentrated revision. Make use too of the tips for revision and sitting your exam to ensure you perform to the best of your ability on the day.

Practice makes perfect. This book should prove an invaluable revision aid and will help you prepare to succeed.

Good luck!

Acknowledgements

Every effort has been made to trace the copyright holders and to obtain their permission for the use of copyright material. Leckie & Leckie will gladly receive information enabling them to rectify any error or omission in subsequent editions.

2000 HIGHER

Official SQA Past Papers: Higher Biology 2000

FOR OFFICIAL USE

Total

X007/301

NATIONAL QUALIFICATIONS 2000

MONDAY, 29 MAY
9.00 AM – 11.30 AM

BIOLOGY HIGHER

Fill in these boxes and read what is printed below.

Full name of centre

Town

Forename(s)

Surname

Date of birth
Day Month Year

Scottish candidate number

Number of seat

SECTION A—Questions 1–30 (30 marks)

Instructions for completion of Section A are given on page two.

SECTIONS B AND C (100 marks)

1. (a) All questions should be attempted.
   (b) It should be noted that in **Section C** questions 1 and 2 each contain a choice.
   (c) Question 14 is on pages 30, 31 and 32. The additional graph paper is on page 33. Pages 32 and 33 are fold-out pages.

2. The questions may be answered in any order but all answers are to be written in the spaces provided in this answer book, and must be written clearly and legibly in ink.

3. Additional space for answers and rough work will be found at the end of the book. If further space is required, supplementary sheets may be obtained from the invigilator and should be inserted inside the **front** cover of this book.

4. The numbers of questions must be clearly inserted with any answers written in the additional space.

5. Rough work, if any should be necessary, should be written in this book and then scored through when the fair copy has been written.

6. Before leaving the examination room you must give this book to the invigilator. If you do not, you may lose all the marks for this paper.

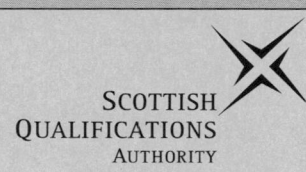

SCOTTISH QUALIFICATIONS AUTHORITY

SECTION A

Read carefully

1. Check that the answer sheet provided is for Biology Higher (Section A).
2. Fill in the details required on the answer sheet.
3. In this section a question is answered by indicating the choice A, B, C or D by a stroke made in **ink** in the appropriate place in the answer sheet—see the sample question below.
4. For each question there is only **one** correct answer.
5. Rough working, if required, should be done only on this question paper—or on the rough working sheet provided—**not** on the answer sheet.
6. At the end of the examination the answer sheet for Section A **must** be placed inside the front cover of this answer book.

Sample Question

Which of the following molecules contains six carbon atoms?

A Pyruvic acid
B Glucose
C Ribulose bisphosphate
D Acetyl co-enzyme A

The correct answer is **B**—glucose. A **heavy** vertical line should be drawn joining the two dots in the appropriate box in the column headed **B** as shown in the example on the answer sheet.

If, after you have recorded your answer, you decide that you have made an error and wish to make a change, you should cancel the original answer and put a vertical stroke in the box you now consider to be correct. Thus, if you want to change an answer D to an answer B, your answer sheet would look like this:

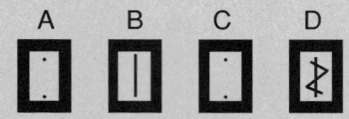

If you want to change back to an answer which has already been scored out, you should enter a tick (✓) to the **right** of the box of your choice, thus:

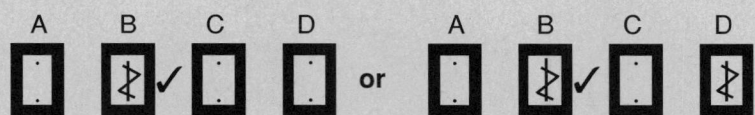

SECTION A

All questions in this section should be attempted.

Answers should be given on the separate answer sheet provided.

1. The graph shows the rates of respiration and photosynthesis in a plant, over a 24 hour period.

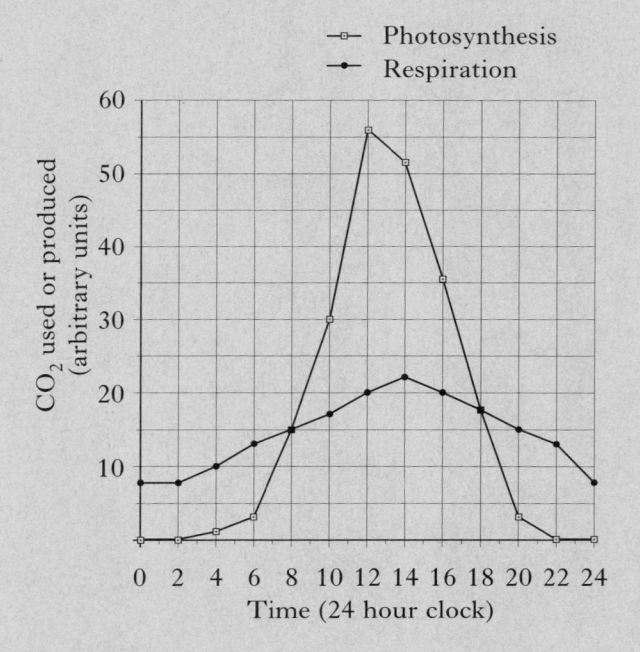

   At which of the following times is there the greatest net production of carbohydrate?

   A 0800 hours
   B 1200 hours
   C 1400 hours
   D 1800 hours

2. The graph shows the effect of varying carbon dioxide concentration on the rate of photosynthesis in a plant.

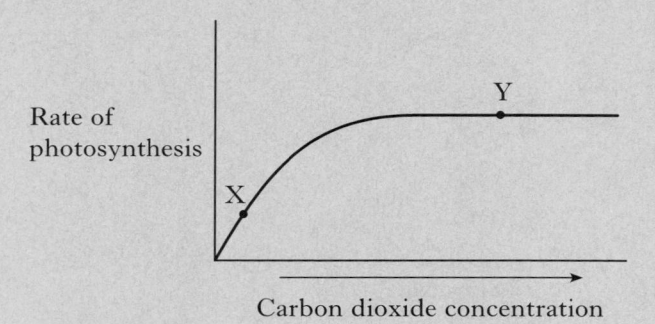

   Which line in the table shows factors which could be limiting the rate of photosynthesis at points X and Y?

	Limiting factor at X	Limiting factor at Y
A	temperature	carbon dioxide concentration
B	light intensity	temperature
C	carbon dioxide concentration	temperature
D	carbon dioxide concentration	carbon dioxide concentration

3. Those cells of seaweed which actively absorb iodide ions from sea water would be expected to have large numbers of

   A mitochondria
   B chloroplasts
   C ribosomes
   D vacuoles.

   [Turn over

4. Which of the following correctly identifies the sequence in which organelles become involved in the production of a hormone for secretion?

   A   Nucleus → Ribosome → Golgi Apparatus → Rough E.R.

   B   Ribosomes → Rough E.R. → Golgi Apparatus → Vesicles

   C   Nucleus → Rough E.R. → Vesicles → Ribosomes

   D   Ribosomes → Vesicles → Rough E.R. → Golgi Apparatus

5. Cyanogenesis in *Trifolium repens* is a defence mechanism against

   A   grazing

   B   bacterial invasion

   C   fungal infection

   D   water loss.

6. Which of the following is **not** a plant response to invasion by other organisms?

   The production of

   A   resin

   B   nicotine

   C   antibodies

   D   tannins.

7. Lysosomes are involved in the defence of the body as they

   A   carry out phagocytosis to engulf bacteria

   B   produce antibodies to destroy viruses

   C   contain lymphocytes

   D   allow phagocytes to digest bacteria.

8. An enzyme and its substrate were incubated with various concentrations of either copper or magnesium salts.

   The time taken for the complete breakdown of the substrate was measured.

   The results are given in the table.

Metal concentration (mol l^{-1})	Time needed to break down substrate (Seconds)	
	Copper salts	Magnesium salts
0	39	39
1×10^{-8}	42	21
1×10^{-6}	380	49
1×10^{-4}	1480	286

   Which line in the table below describes correctly the effects of high concentrations of these metals on enzyme activity?

	High concentration of copper salts	High concentration of magnesium salts
A	promoted	promoted
B	promoted	inhibited
C	inhibited	inhibited
D	inhibited	promoted

Questions 9 and 10 refer to the information below.

In tomato plants, dominant allele **P** determines purple stem and allele **p** determines green stem. In addition, dominant allele **F** determines a cut-edged leaf and allele **f** determines a smooth-edged leaf.

The following table shows two crosses of tomato plants.

PARENT CROSSES	NUMBER OF PROGENY			
	Purple and cut	Purple and smooth	Green and cut	Green and smooth
1 Purple, cut × purple, smooth	219	207	64	71
2 Purple, cut × green, cut	722	231	0	0

9. What are the most probable genotypes for the parents in cross 1?

   A PpFF × PPff
   B PpFF × Ppff
   C PpFf × PPff
   D PpFf × Ppff

10. What are the most probable genotypes for the parents in cross 2?

    A PPFf × ppFF
    B PPFf × ppFf
    C PpFf × ppFF
    D PpFf × ppFf

11. Huntington's chorea is a non-sex-linked dominant condition in which muscle coordination and mental abilities are gradually lost. Usually the symptoms do not appear until the person is approaching middle age.

    A woman's father is heterozygous for this condition. Her mother is normal. What are the chances of her inheriting this condition?

    A 1 in 1
    B 1 in 2
    C 1 in 3
    D 1 in 4

12. Which of the following describes the chromosome complement of a white blood cell?

    A Polyploid
    B Diploid
    C Haploid
    D Nil

13. The following table refers to the mass of DNA in certain human body cells.

Cell type	Mass of DNA/cell ($\times 10^{-12}$ g)
liver	6·6
lung	6·6
P	3·3
Q	0·0

From the information in the table, cell types P and Q are, respectively

A a kidney cell and an ovum
B a nerve cell and a mature red blood cell
C a mature red blood cell and an ovum
D an ovum and a mature red blood cell.

14. The table below shows the number of chromosomes in human gametes from both normal and abnormal meiosis.

An autosome is any chromosome other than a sex chromosome.

Gamete	Number of autosomes	Type of sex chromosome
A	23	X
B	22	X
C	22	Y
D	23	Y

Which ovum, when fertilised with a normal sperm, will result in a child with Down's Syndrome?

15. The diagram below represents the areas of interbreeding of 4 groups of birds. Interbreeding takes place in the shaded areas.

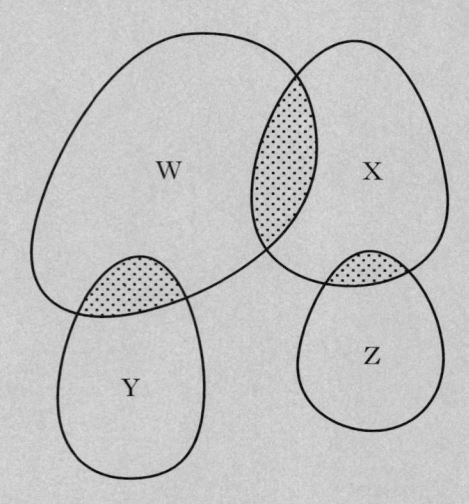

How many species are present?

A 1
B 2
C 3
D 4

16. In an investigation into the population size of peppered moths, 50 moths were captured in a woodland area, marked and released. One day later, another 50 moths were captured and 10 of these were found to be marked.

All the marked moths had survived in the area during the 24 hour period. What is the estimated moth population in the woodland area?

A 60
B 90
C 250
D 500

17. Which of the following adaptations are likely to occur in a desert mammal?

A Short loops of Henlé and a low concentration of ADH
B Short loops of Henlé and a high concentration of ADH
C Long loops of Henlé and a low concentration of ADH
D Long loops of Henlé and a high concentration of ADH

18. Which of the following is an example of competition within a species?

A Poppies growing amongst wheat
B Maize plants growing in a field
C Bracken growing around seedling pine trees
D Rabbits and sheep feeding on grass in the same field

19. Which of the following statements about habituation is correct?

A It is a temporary change in behaviour.
B It occurs only in young animals.
C It is an example of social behaviour.
D It is a permanent change in behaviour.

20. Two plants of different species had their carbon dioxide (CO$_2$) uptake and output measured in relation to light intensity. The results are shown below.

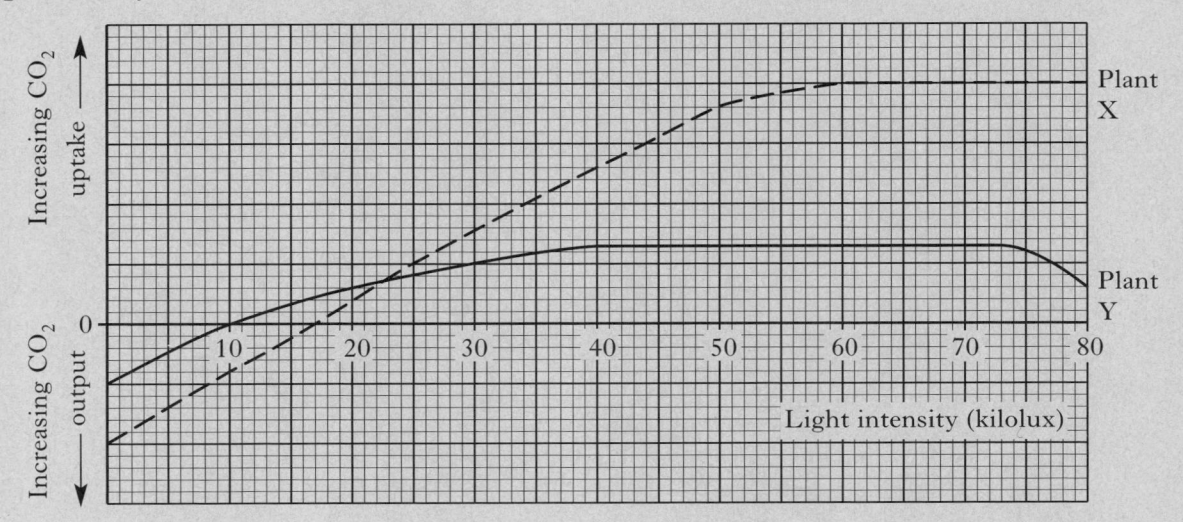

Which of the conclusions in the table below would be a correct interpretation of the graphs?

	Type of plant	Light intensity at which Compensation Point is reached
A	Plant X is a shade plant.	17 kilolux
B	Plant X is a sun plant.	60 kilolux
C	Plant Y is a sun plant.	40 kilolux
D	Plant Y is a shade plant.	10 kilolux

Questions 21 and 22 refer to the diagram of a transverse section through a dicotyledon stem shown below.

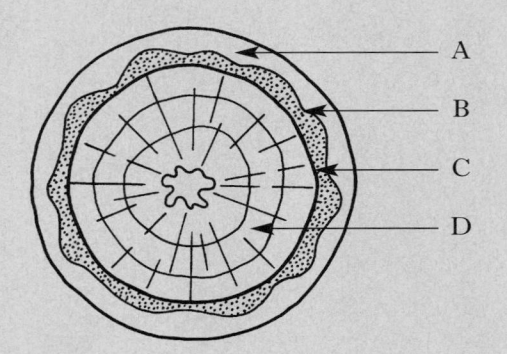

21. In the diagram of a transverse section of a dicotyledon stem shown above, where is a meristematic layer to be found?

22. In which region of the stem would the structure shown in the diagram below be found?

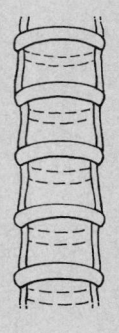

23. Which of the following plant cells is **not** formed as a result of differentiation?

A Cambium cell

B Companion cell

C Phloem sieve tube

D Xylem vessel

[Turn over

24. Part of the *E. coli* chromosome is shown in the diagram below.

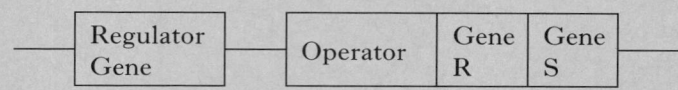

| Regulator Gene | Operator | Gene R | Gene S |

The product of the regulator gene normally binds with the operator. If a mutation occurs in the regulator gene such that its product can no longer bind with the operator, which of the following occurs?

A Transcription of genes R and S only when the appropriate substrate is present

B No transcription of genes R and S at any time

C Continuous transcription of genes R and S

D Intermittent transcription of genes R and S

25. An investigation into the influence of different concentrations of IAA on the development of certain plant organs was carried out. The growth-inhibiting or growth-promoting effects are shown below.

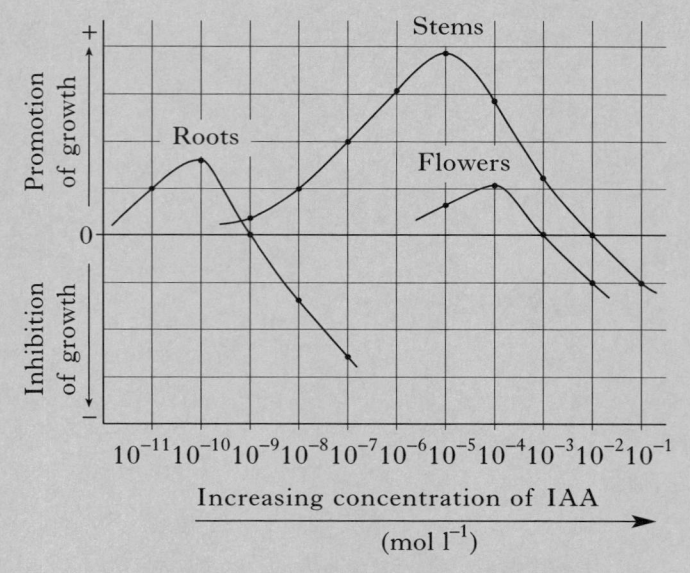

The graph shows that an IAA concentration of

A 10^{-3} mol l^{-1} promotes flowering and stem growth

B 10^{-5} mol l^{-1} causes increase in stem length and flower production

C 10^{-7} mol l^{-1} increases growth in roots and stems

D 10^{-9} mol l^{-1} inhibits stem growth and promotes root growth.

26. The flow diagram below outlines the processes which occur in the human body to speed up the metabolic rate.

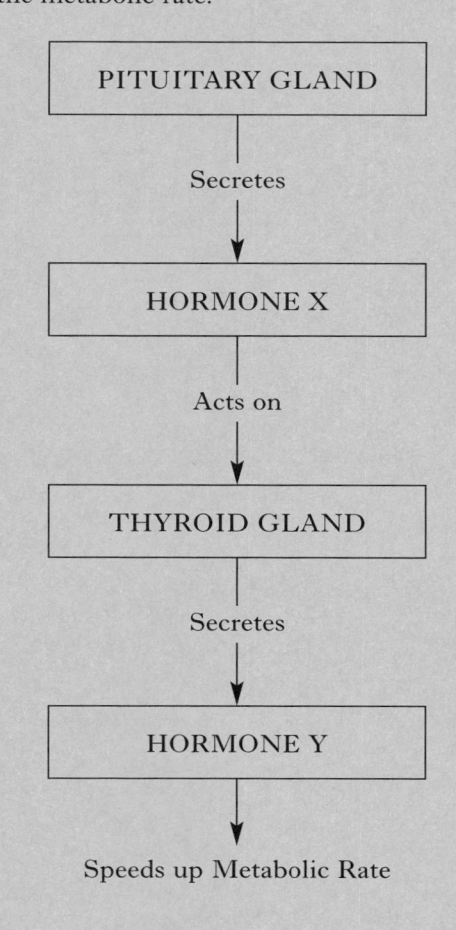

PITUITARY GLAND
↓ Secretes
HORMONE X
↓ Acts on
THYROID GLAND
↓ Secretes
HORMONE Y
↓
Speeds up Metabolic Rate

Hormones X and Y are

	X	Y
A	Thyroid Stimulating Hormone (TSH)	Thyroxine
B	Growth Hormone	Thyroid Stimulating Hormone (TSH)
C	Thyroxine	Thyroid Stimulating Hormone (TSH)
D	Thyroid Stimulating Hormone (TSH)	Growth Hormone

27. In a germinating barley grain, gibberellic acid stimulates the production of

A soluble sugar by the endosperm

B amylase by the endosperm

C soluble sugar by the aleurone layer

D amylase by the aleurone layer.

28. The table below gives information concerning three macro-elements X, Y and Z.

Macro-elements	Symptom of deficiency	Role of the macro-element
X	Chlorotic leaves Reduced growth	Required for chlorophyll production
Y	Reduced growth Leaf bases red	Required for ATP and nucleic acids
Z	Chlorotic leaves Reduced growth	Formation of proteins and nucleic acids

Which of the following correctly identifies X, Y and Z?

	X	Y	Z
A	Magnesium	Nitrogen	Phosphorus
B	Nitrogen	Potassium	Magnesium
C	Magnesium	Phosphorus	Nitrogen
D	Nitrogen	Magnesium	Potassium

29. Drinking a large volume of water will lead to

A increased production of ADH and kidney tubules becoming more permeable

B decreased production of ADH and kidney tubules becoming more permeable

C decreased production of ADH and kidney tubules becoming less permeable

D increased production of ADH and kidney tubules becoming less permeable.

30. The graph below shows the variation in prey and predator numbers recorded over a ten week period.

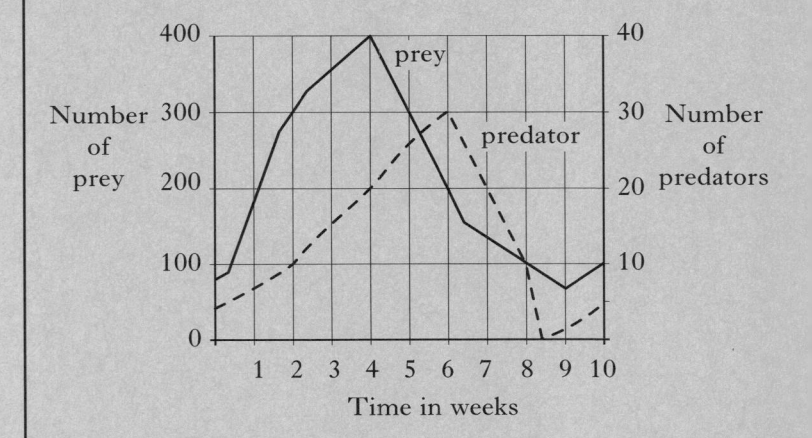

In which week is the prey to predator ratio largest?

A Week 2

B Week 4

C Week 6

D Week 8

Candidates are reminded that the answer sheet MUST be returned INSIDE the front cover of this answer book.

[Turn over for Section B on *Page ten*

SECTION B

All questions in this section should be attempted.

1. The pathway below represents an outline of stages in respiration in a mammalian cell.

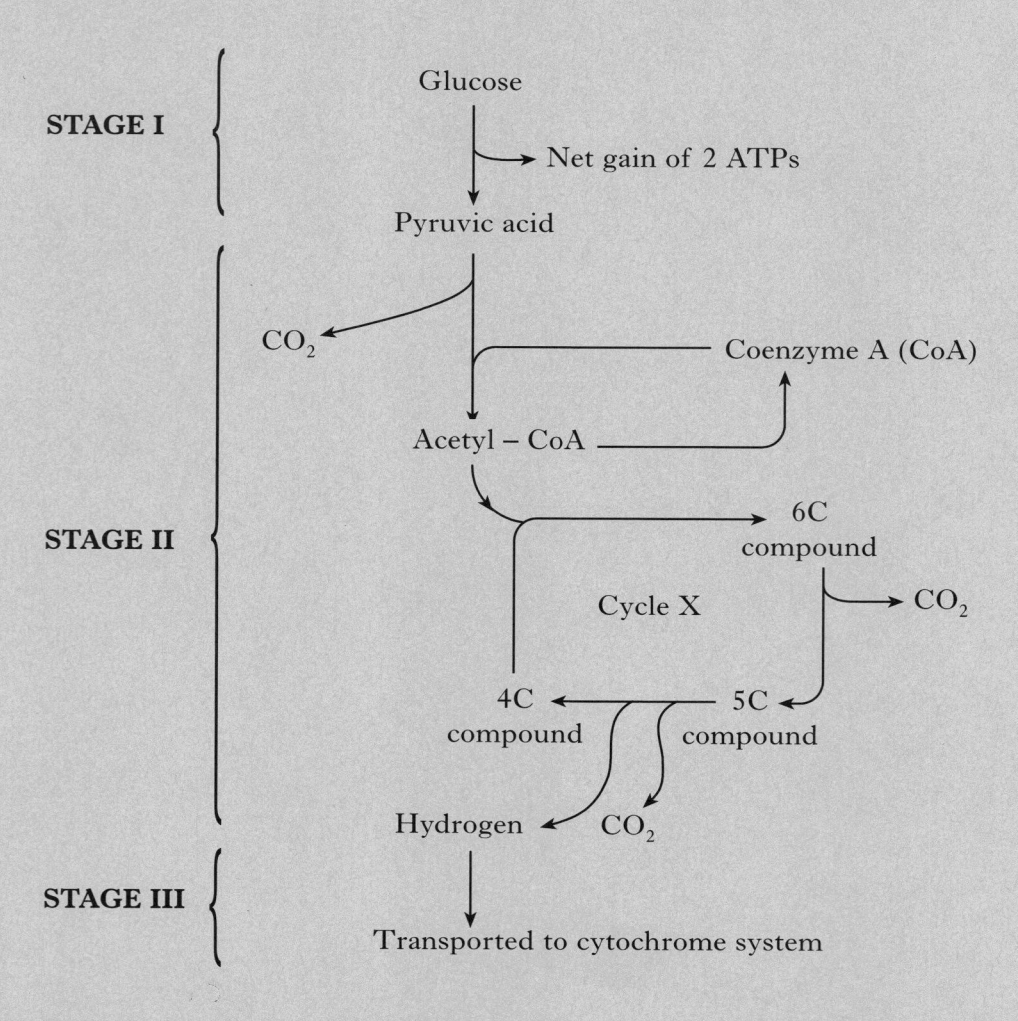

STAGE I
- Glucose → Net gain of 2 ATPs → Pyruvic acid

STAGE II
- Pyruvic acid → CO$_2$ + Coenzyme A (CoA) → Acetyl–CoA
- Acetyl–CoA → 6C compound → CO$_2$ → 5C compound → CO$_2$ + 4C compound (Cycle X) → Hydrogen

STAGE III
- Hydrogen → Transported to cytochrome system

(a) Complete the table below by inserting the number of carbon atoms present in each substance.

Substance	Number of carbon atoms
Glucose	
Pyruvic acid	
Acetyl group	

2

(b) Explain why the gain of 2ATPs in **STAGE I** is described as being a **net** gain.

_____

_____

1

1. (continued)

(c) Name cycle X in **STAGE II**.

Name _____ 1

(d) Name the carrier that transfers hydrogen to the cytochrome system.

Name _____ 1

(e) Name the final hydrogen acceptor in **STAGE III**.

Name _____ 1

[Turn over

2. (a) Slices of beetroot, rhubarb and celery tissues were immersed in sugar solutions of different concentrations. After 30 minutes the number of plasmolysed cells in a sample of 50 cells was counted under a microscope.

Concentration of sugar solution ($mol\,l^{-1}$)	Number of plasmolysed cells in a sample of 50 cells after 30 minutes		
	Beetroot tissue	Rhubarb tissue	Celery tissue
0·30	0	10	5
0·35	4	16	8
0·40	10	25	14
0·45	20	40	30
0·50	35	45	40
0·55	50	50	50

(i) From the table, identify the solute concentration of the cell contents of rhubarb tissue in which 50% of the tissue cells show plasmolysis.

_____ $mol\,l^{-1}$

(ii) Explain how the results for celery tissue at a concentration of $0·35\ mol\,l^{-1}$ suggest that the cells do not all have the same cell sap concentration.

_____

_____

(iii) Which of the tissues has cells with the highest solute concentration?

Tissue _____

(iv) From the results, calculate the percentage increase in the number of plasmolysed cells which would occur in beetroot tissue when moved from a $0·45\ mol\,l^{-1}$ to a $0·50\ mol\,l^{-1}$ sugar solution.

Space for calculation

Answer _____ %

2. (continued)

(b) The descriptions in the list below refer to either the cell wall or the cell membrane.

Complete the table, using the letter **W** for descriptions of the cell wall and **M** for descriptions of the cell membrane.

Description	Letter
Destroyed by boiling	
Made up of fibres	
Fully permeable	
A fluid mosaic	
Contains proteins	

(c) The graph shows the effect of change in the oxygen concentration on the rate of absorption of potassium ions from solution by the roots of barley seedlings.

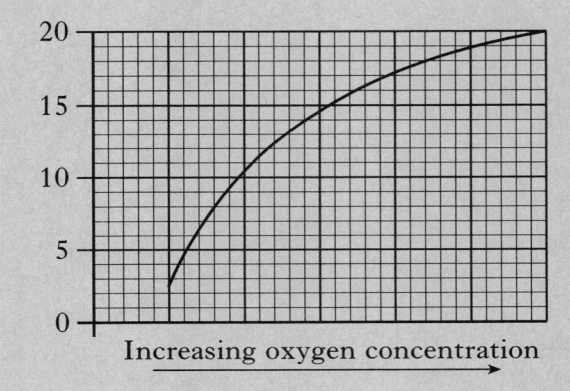

Account for the effect of increased oxygen concentration on the absorption of potassium ions from solution.

_____

_____

_____

[Turn over

3. (a) In an investigation into the sequence of reactions that occur in photosynthesis, unicellular green algae were kept in the dark for 24 hours and then exposed to light for varying periods. After each period of illumination an extract of the algal cells was obtained. The chromatograms developed from these extracts are shown below together with the length of the period of illumination.

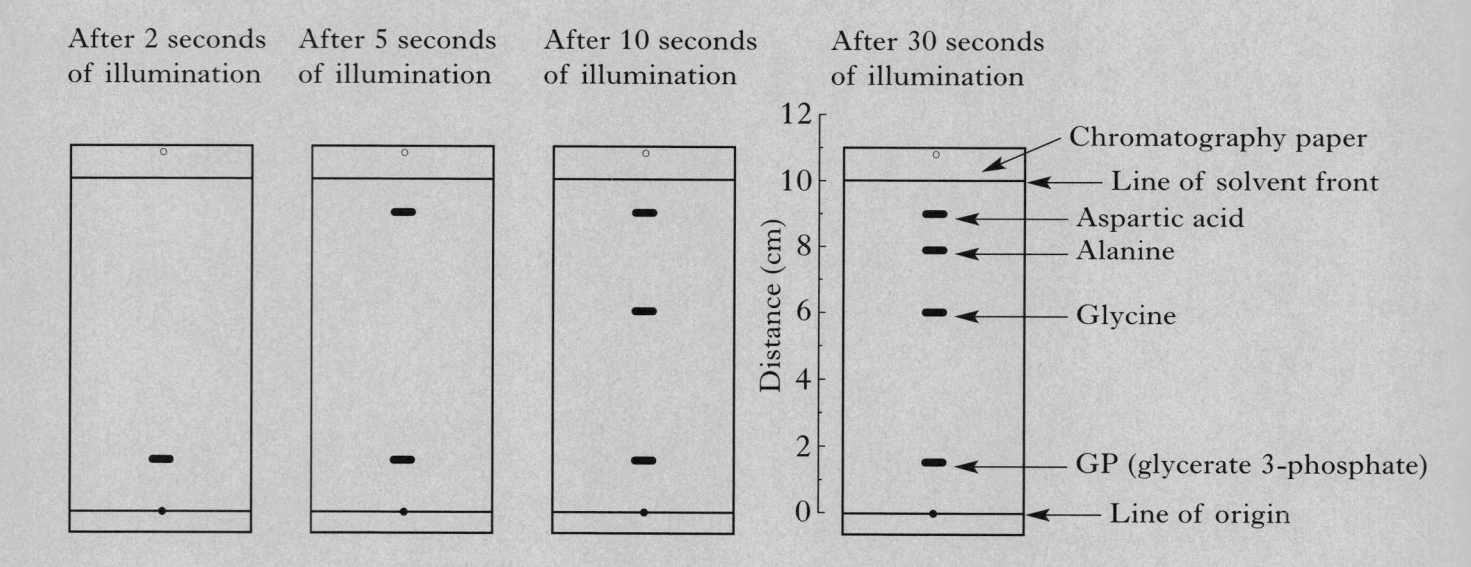

(i) From the chromatograms, state the sequence in which these chemical compounds were formed.

Sequence _____ → _____ → _____ → _____ 1

(ii) The Rf value of a compound can be calculated from a chromatogram and then used to identify the compound. The formula for calculating the Rf value is shown below.

$$Rf\ value = \frac{\text{Distance travelled by compound from origin}}{\text{Distance travelled by solvent from origin}}$$

From the chromatogram, using the formula, calculate the Rf value of glycine.

Space for calculation

Rf value for glycine = _____ 1

3. (continued)

(b) The graph below shows the relative concentrations of glycerate 3-phosphate (GP) and ribulose 1, 5-bisphosphate (RuBP) in a chloroplast during changes in light and dark conditions.

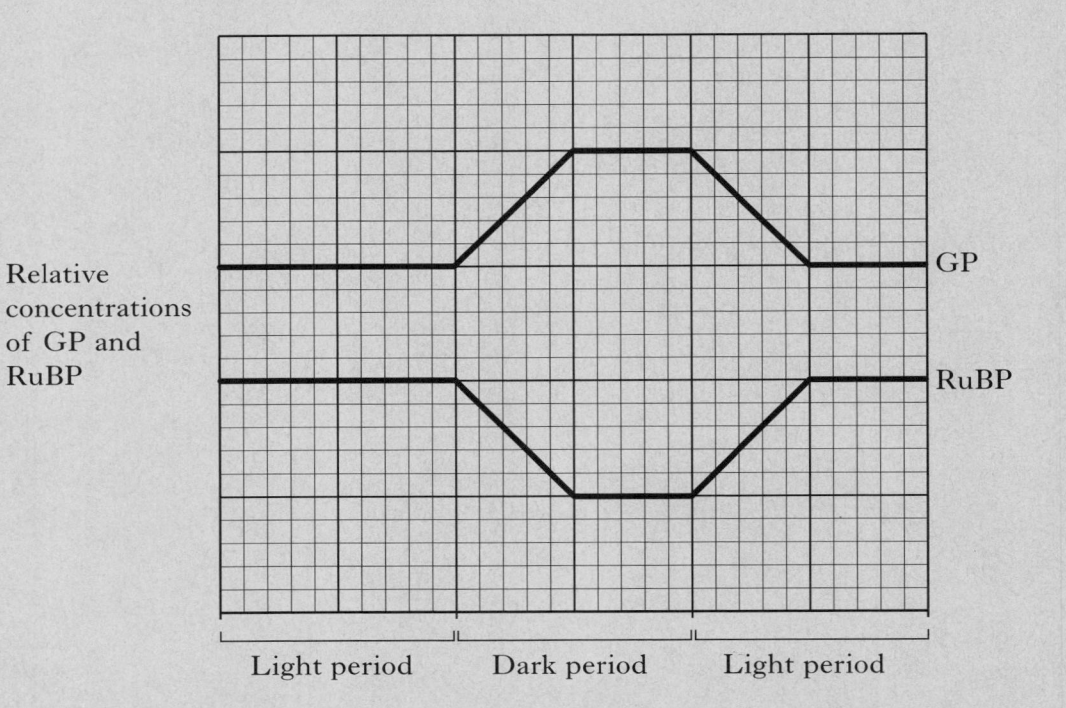

(i) What evidence from the graph supports the statement that GP can be converted to RuBP in the light?

_____

_____ 1

(ii) Name the **two** chemical compounds produced in the light dependent stage that are required for the conversion of GP to RuBP.

Compound 1 _____ Compound 2 _____ 1

(iii) Other than being converted to RuBP, GP is also converted to a 6 carbon sugar. Name this 6 carbon sugar.

Name _____ 1

(iv) Within which region of the chloroplast does the inter-conversion of GP and RuBP occur?

Region _____ 1

[Turn over

4. (a) The diagram below represents the four different nucleotides of DNA. The bases of the nucleotides are bonded in pairs.

(i) Name the type of bond which links the base of one nucleotide to the base of another.

Name _____

(ii) **On the diagram**:

1 insert the appropriate letters or names of the four different nucleotides;

2 draw lines to show how adjacent nucleotides are bonded in a DNA molecule.

(b) Complete the table below to show structural differences between the nucleic acids DNA and RNA.

| | Type of nucleic acid ||
Structure	DNA	RNA
Number of strands present		
Type of sugar in nucleotide		

4. **(continued)**

   (c) The diagram below shows part of one strand of a DNA molecule and the results of four different types of gene mutation which can occur within this molecule.

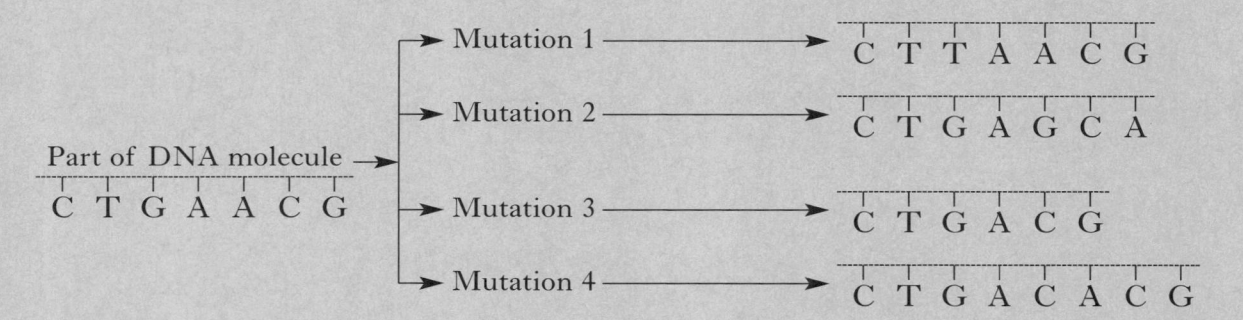

   Part of DNA molecule → C T G A A C G

   → Mutation 1 → C T T A A C G
   → Mutation 2 → C T G A G C A
   → Mutation 3 → C T G A C G
   → Mutation 4 → C T G A C A C G

   Complete the table below by naming the type of gene mutation which has occurred in each case.

Mutation number	Type of gene mutation
1	
2	
3	
4	

   (d) Name **one** mutagenic agent.

   _____

   (e) Haemophilia in humans results from a gene mutation.

   The allele for haemophilia (**h**) is sex-linked and recessive to the normal allele (**H**) for blood clotting.

   The family tree below shows inheritance of the condition.

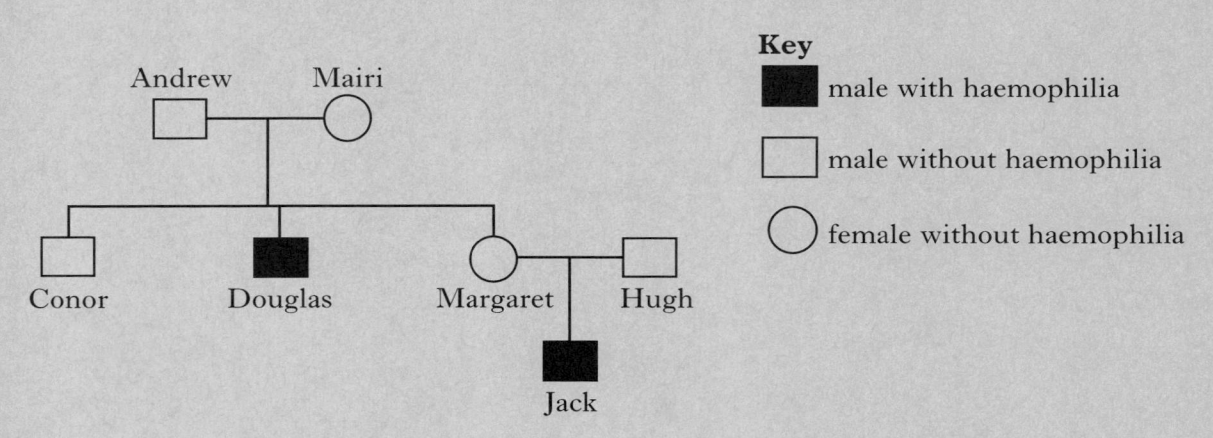

   Key
   ■ male with haemophilia
   □ male without haemophilia
   ○ female without haemophilia

   Give the genotype of each of the following individuals.

   Conor _____ Douglas _____ Margaret _____

5. The diagram below shows the structure of a virus that invades and replicates within plant cells.

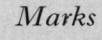

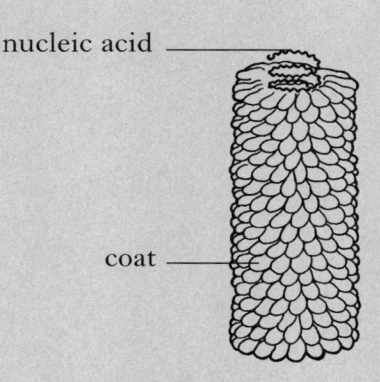

nucleic acid

coat

(a) Name the type of chemical substance that forms the viral coat.

Name _____ **1**

(b) Stages in the invasion of a plant cell by a virus are listed below.

Using the appropriate letters, place the stages in the correct sequence.

Letter	Stages
A	Assembly of new viruses
B	Synthesis of viral coat
C	Entry of viral nucleic acid into cell
D	Replication of viral nucleic acid

Sequence ____ → ____ → ____ → ____ **1**

(c) The sequence below shows transmission of a virus through **two** generations.

1 Virus infects a plant cell.
2 First generation of viruses released.
3 New plant cells infected.
4 Second generation of viruses released.

The figures for transmission success of the virus to new plant cells are shown below.

50 viruses are released from any infected plant cell.
30% of released viruses infect new plant cells.

If a single virus infected a plant cell, calculate the number of viruses expected to be released in the second generation.

Space for calculation

Number _____ **1**

6. Read these statements about enzymes and answer the questions which follow.

1. Enzymes play a vital role in the life of all organisms. Their activity can be affected by environmental factors such as the presence of lead.
2. Enzymes are proteins and are coded for by genes.
3. Occasionally a gene mutation occurs and the effect of this is the production of an abnormal enzyme.
4. An abnormal enzyme may cause a block in a metabolic pathway.
5. Certain bacteria produce the enzyme β-galactosidase which breaks down lactose.
6. Production of this enzyme is normally prevented by the activity of a regulator gene.

(a) What is the effect of lead referred to in statement 1?

_____

_____ 1

(b) To which class of proteins do enzymes belong (statement 2)?

_____ 1

(c) Explain how a gene mutation would lead to production of an abnormal enzyme (statement 3).

_____

_____ 1

(d) Explain how the activity of the regulator gene has the effect described in statement 6.

_____

_____ 1

(e) Which statements describe the cause of a disorder such as phenylketonuria?

_____ 1

[Turn over

7. The diagram below represents a stage in the process of meiosis.

The letters E or e, F or f and G or g show the positions of the alleles of three genes.

Homologous pairs of chromosomes align and form points of contact as shown by X and Y.

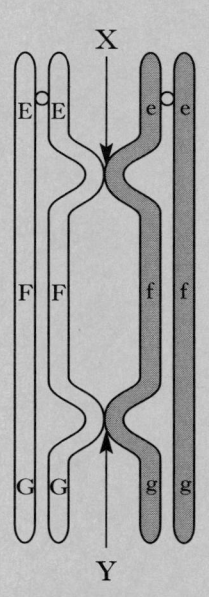

(a) What name is given to points X and Y?

_____ 1

(b) Crossing over may take place at points X and Y.

In the table below tick (✓) the boxes to identify which combinations of alleles would result from crossing over at point X only, and crossing over at both points X and Y.

Combination of alleles	Crossing over at point X only	Crossing over at points X and Y
eFg		
EfG		
eFG		
Efg		
EFg		
efG		

2

(c) Crossing over is a feature of meiosis that leads to variation.

Name **one** other feature of meiosis that leads to variation.

_____

_____ 1

7. (continued)

(d) In a certain organism, the genes P, Q, R and S are located on the same chromosome. The table below shows the frequency of recombination between different pairs of genes.

Gene pairs	Frequency of recombination %
P and Q	8
P and R	14
Q and R	22
Q and S	4
S and P	12

Use the information in the above table to show the positions of genes P, Q, R and S in relation to each other on the chromosome diagram below.

Chromosome --

[Turn over

8. (*a*) A salmon was transferred from fresh water to salt water.
The graph below shows the changes in the drinking rate of the salmon.

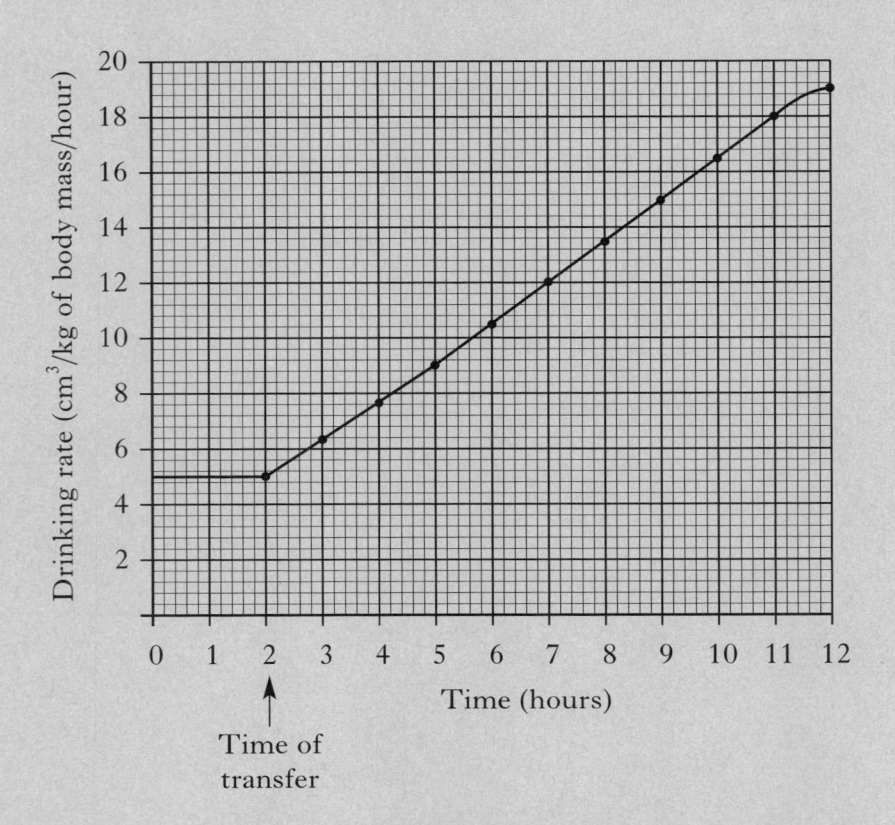

(i) Calculate the volume of water drunk by a salmon weighing 2·5 kg over the two hour period before it was transferred to salt water.

Space for calculation

_____ cm³   **1**

(ii) Calculate the percentage increase in the drinking rate nine hours after transfer.

Space for calculation

_____ %   **1**

(iii) Describe the activity of the chloride secretory cells of the gills while the salmon is in the fresh water environment.

_____

_____   **1**

8. (a) (continued)

   (iv) Complete the following sentences by **underlining** one of the words from each pair.

   When the salmon is in salt water, water {leaves / enters} by osmosis.

   The reason for this is that its tissues are {hypertonic / hypotonic} to the salt water.

   (v) In the table below tick (✓) the boxes which show the changes in kidney function which occur when the salmon is transferred to salt water.

Kidney function	Increase	Decrease	Stays the same
Rate of filtration			
Rate of production of urine			

(b) The diagram below represents a cross section through a leaf that has sunken stomata.

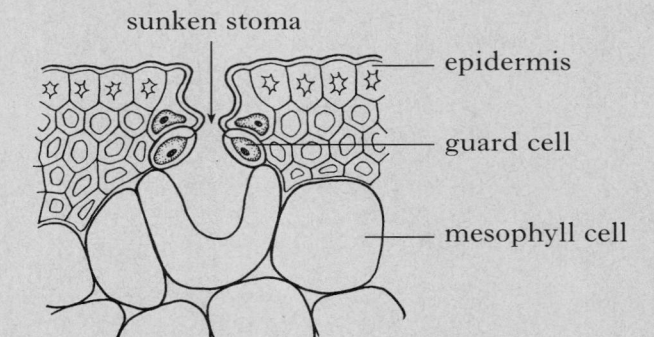

   (i) Describe the conditions of the environment in which plants with sunken stomata may be found.
   Explain how this adaptation would be advantageous to survival in these conditions.

   Conditions _____

   Explanation _____

   (ii) Explain the effect of an increase in turgor of the guard cells on the rate of transpiration.

9. The apparatus shown below was used to measure the rate of transpiration of a leafy twig at different temperatures.

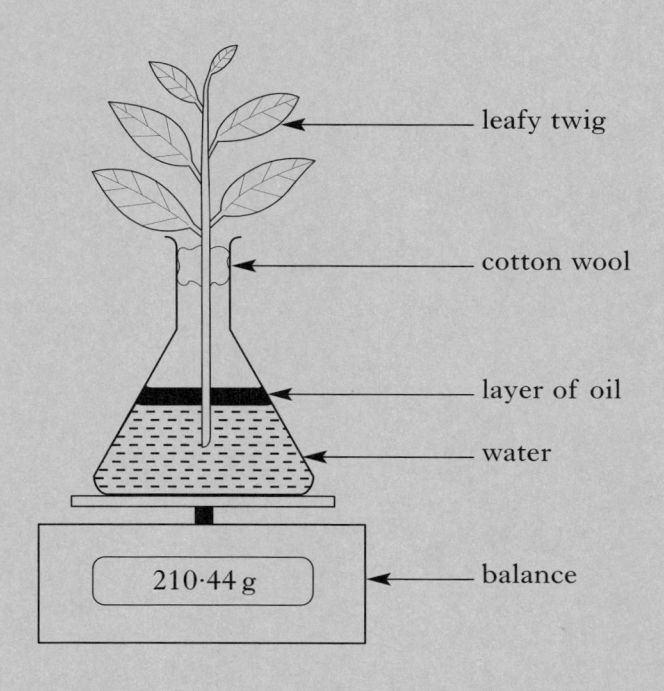

- leafy twig
- cotton wool
- layer of oil
- water
- balance

210·44 g

The changes in mass recorded can be used to calculate the mass of water lost in transpiration over a 10 minute period of time.

(a) Explain why the twig was cut off under water when the apparatus was being set up.

_____

_____ 1

(b) The apparatus was left at each temperature for 15 minutes before starting to measure the transpiration rate.

Explain why this precaution was good experimental procedure.

_____

_____ 1

(c) Identify **one** environmental factor that must be kept the same at each temperature in order to make the results obtained valid.

Explain why this factor must be kept constant.

Environmental factor _____

Explanation _____

_____ 1

9. (continued)

The table below shows the results of the investigation.

Temperature (°C)	Change in mass per 10 minutes (g)
5	1·5
10	3·0
15	4·5
20	5·5
25	6·0

(d) Using the results, plot a line graph of change in mass per 10 minutes against temperature in the grid below.

(Additional graph paper, if required, can be found on page 33.)

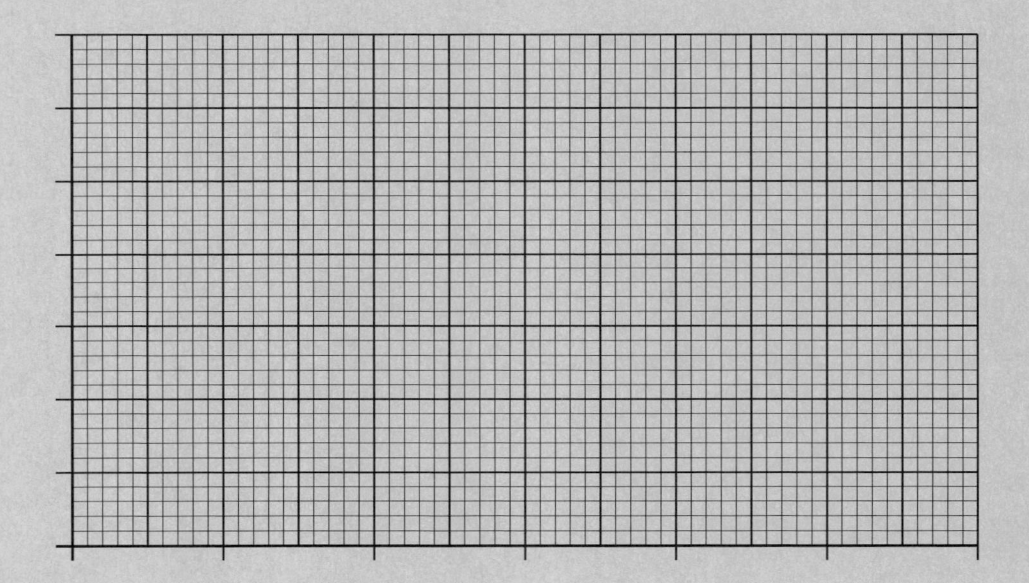

(e) From the results, predict the change in mass for 10 minutes at 30 °C and justify your prediction.

Predicted change in mass _____

Justification _____

_____

[Turn over

10. Indole acetic acid (IAA) and gibberellic acid (GA) are plant growth substances which have effects on the growth and development of flowering plants.

Location	Role of IAA
shoot tip	

Location	Role of IAA
ovary of fertilised flower	

Location	Role of GA
internode	

(a) Complete the boxes above to describe the roles of IAA and GA in the locations shown in the diagram. **2**

(b) Give **one** application of a plant growth substance in horticultural practice. **1**

(c) A change in the photoperiod can initiate the flowering process.

  (i) What is meant by the term photoperiod? **1**

  (ii) State **one** way in which a change in photoperiod affects behaviour in birds. **1**

11. After an area of farmland was abandoned it was colonised initially by herbs and grasses. In the following 80 years there were changes in the plant community as shown in the graphs below. Changes in the depth of organic material in the soil are also shown.

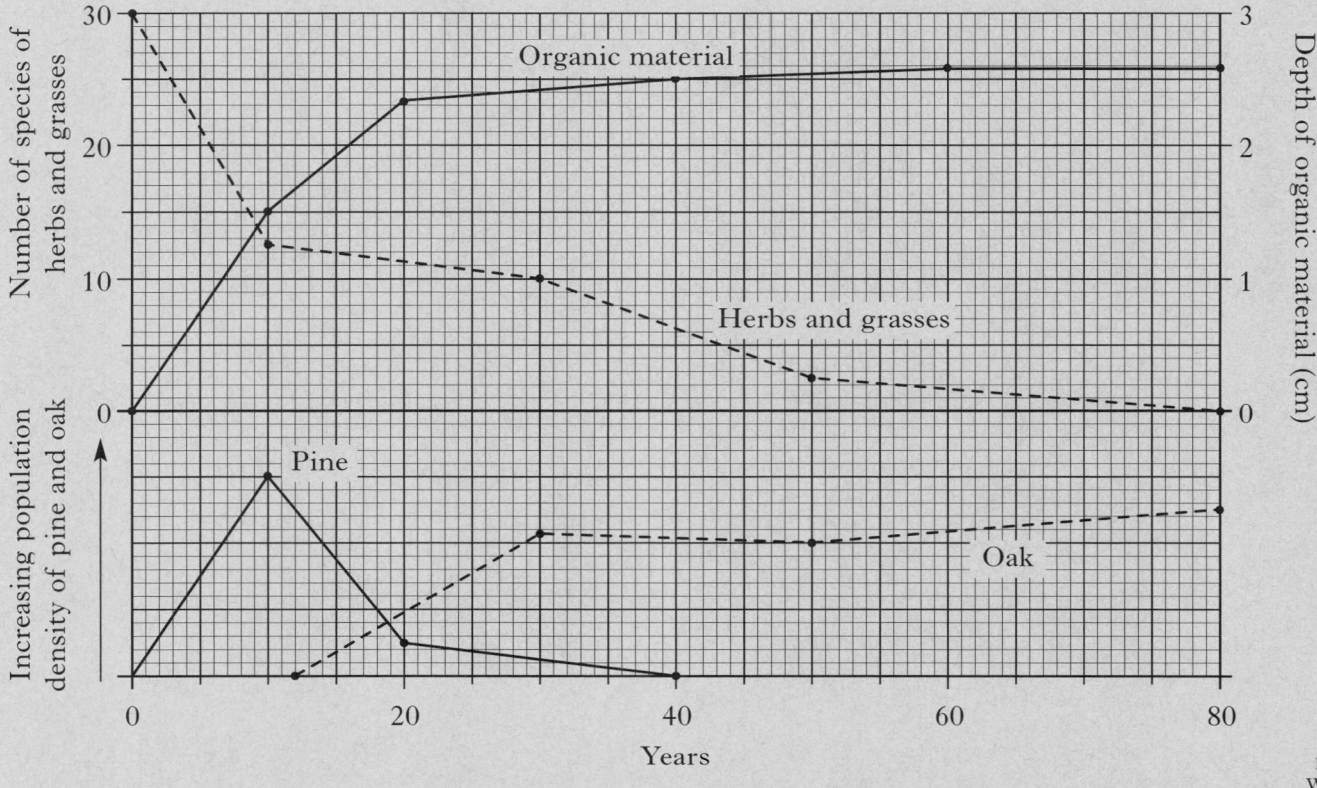

(a) What evidence in the data indicates that succession has taken place?

_____

_____ **1**

(b) Oak seeds can only germinate successfully if there is enough organic material to protect them from drying out.

On the basis of the data given, what is the minimum depth of organic material required by the oak seeds?

Depth _____ cm   **1**

(c) Oak woodland forms the final community in this succession.

State the name given to this community and describe a feature of such a community.

Name _____

Feature _____

_____ **2**

12. Until the 1970s, whales in the Antarctic Ocean were hunted as a source of food and other raw materials. Amongst those hunted were the Blue whale (20–30 metres long), Fin whale (15–25 metres long), Sei whale (10–15 metres long) and Minke whale (7–10 metres long).

The profit from larger whales is greater than from smaller whales.

Changes in whale population can be monitored by examining records of the number of whales caught each year. The information is shown in the table below.

Year	Number of whales caught (thousands)			
	Blue	Fin	Sei	Minke
1930	27	10	0	0
1940	11	18	0	0
1955	3	6	8	0
1965	0	0	18	0
1975	0	0	2	12

(a) Whalers targeted less profitable species of whale when the numbers of the more profitable species declined.

What evidence in the data supports this statement?

_____

_____

(b) (i) Wild populations can be monitored because of their importance as a source of food or raw materials.

State **one** other reason why wild populations are monitored.

_____

_____

(ii) Name **two** density dependent factors which may affect the numbers in a wild population.

Factor 1 _____

Factor 2 _____

13. The list below shows some changes which occur in animals as a result of changes in body temperature.

A	fall in body temperature	E	increase in metabolic rate
B	increase in sweat production	F	erection of hair
C	decrease in metabolic rate	G	constriction of blood vessels
D	hair flattening	H	decrease in sweat production

The diagram below shows part of the control system for body temperature in a mammal.

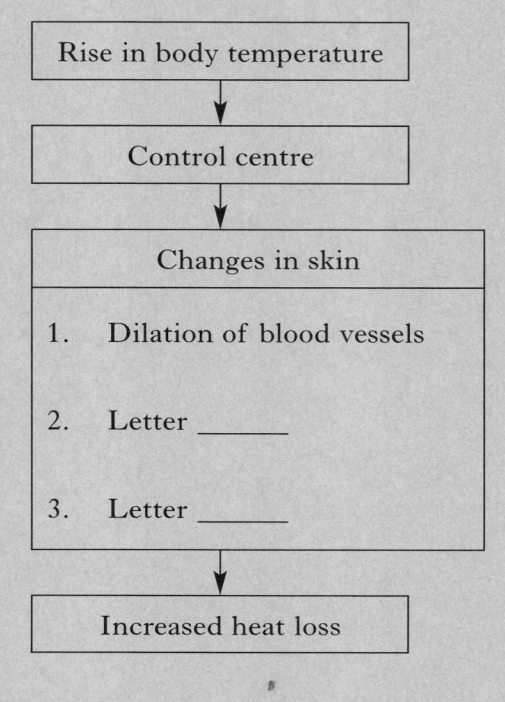

```
        Rise in body temperature
                  ↓
            Control centre
                  ↓
         ┌────────────────────┐
         │  Changes in skin   │
         │                    │
         │ 1. Dilation of blood vessels │
         │                    │
         │ 2. Letter _____    │
         │                    │
         │ 3. Letter _____    │
         └────────────────────┘
                  ↓
          Increased heat loss
```

(a) Complete the diagram by inserting the appropriate letters from the list to show the changes which occur in the skin as a result of a rise in body temperature.

(b) Choose a letter from the list to show the effect of an increase in environmental temperature in an ectotherm.

Letter _____

(c) State how instructions are passed from the control centre to the skin.

_____

[Turn over

14. When the concentration of glucose in the blood rises, there is an increase in the concentration of insulin in the blood. As the insulin concentration increases, the rate of glucose uptake by liver cells increases.

These relationships are shown in **Graph 1** and **Graph 2**.

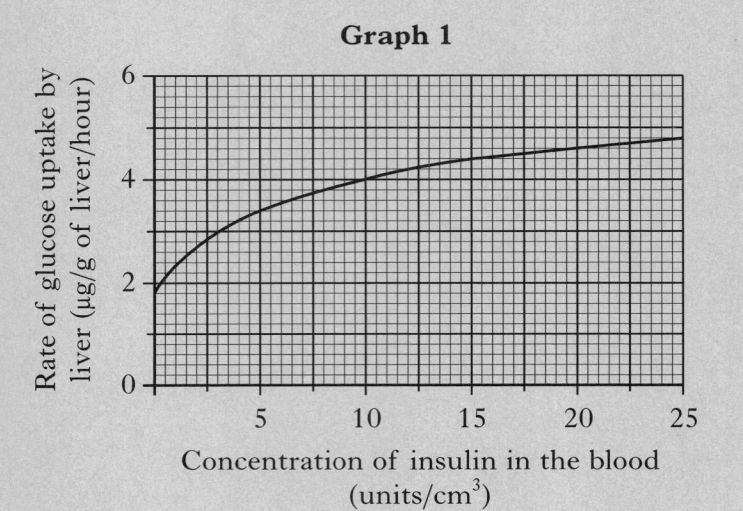

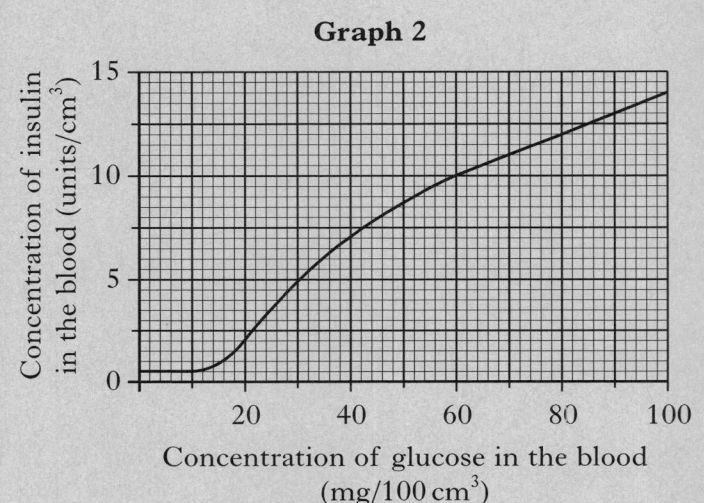

Graph 1

Rate of glucose uptake by liver (μg/g of liver/hour) vs Concentration of insulin in the blood (units/cm³)

Graph 2

Concentration of insulin in the blood (units/cm³) vs Concentration of glucose in the blood (mg/100 cm³)

(a) From **Graph 1**, which change in the concentration of insulin in the blood caused the greatest increase in the rate of glucose uptake by the liver?

Tick (✓) the correct box.

From 0–5 units/cm³ ☐ From 5–10 units/cm³ ☐

From 10–15 units/cm³ ☐ From 15–20 units/cm³ ☐

(b) The volume of blood in a normal, healthy individual is 5 litres.

From **Graph 2**, calculate the mass of glucose present in the blood at an insulin concentration which remains constant at 10 units/cm³.

Space for calculation

_____ mg

(c) From **Graph 1**, calculate the percentage change in the rate of glucose uptake by the liver when the concentration of insulin in the blood increases from 10 units/cm³ to 20 units/cm³.

Space for calculation

_____ %

[Question 14 continues on *Page thirty-one* and fold-out *Page thirty-two*

14. (continued)

(d) From **Graphs 2** and **1**, calculate the rate of glucose uptake by the liver when the concentration of glucose in the blood is 60 mg/100 cm^3.

Space for calculation

_____ µg/g of liver/hour   1

(e) What happens to glucose which is taken up by liver cells?

_____   1

Graph 3 shows the changes in concentration of glucose in the blood of an individual with a normal pancreas and one with a defective pancreas.

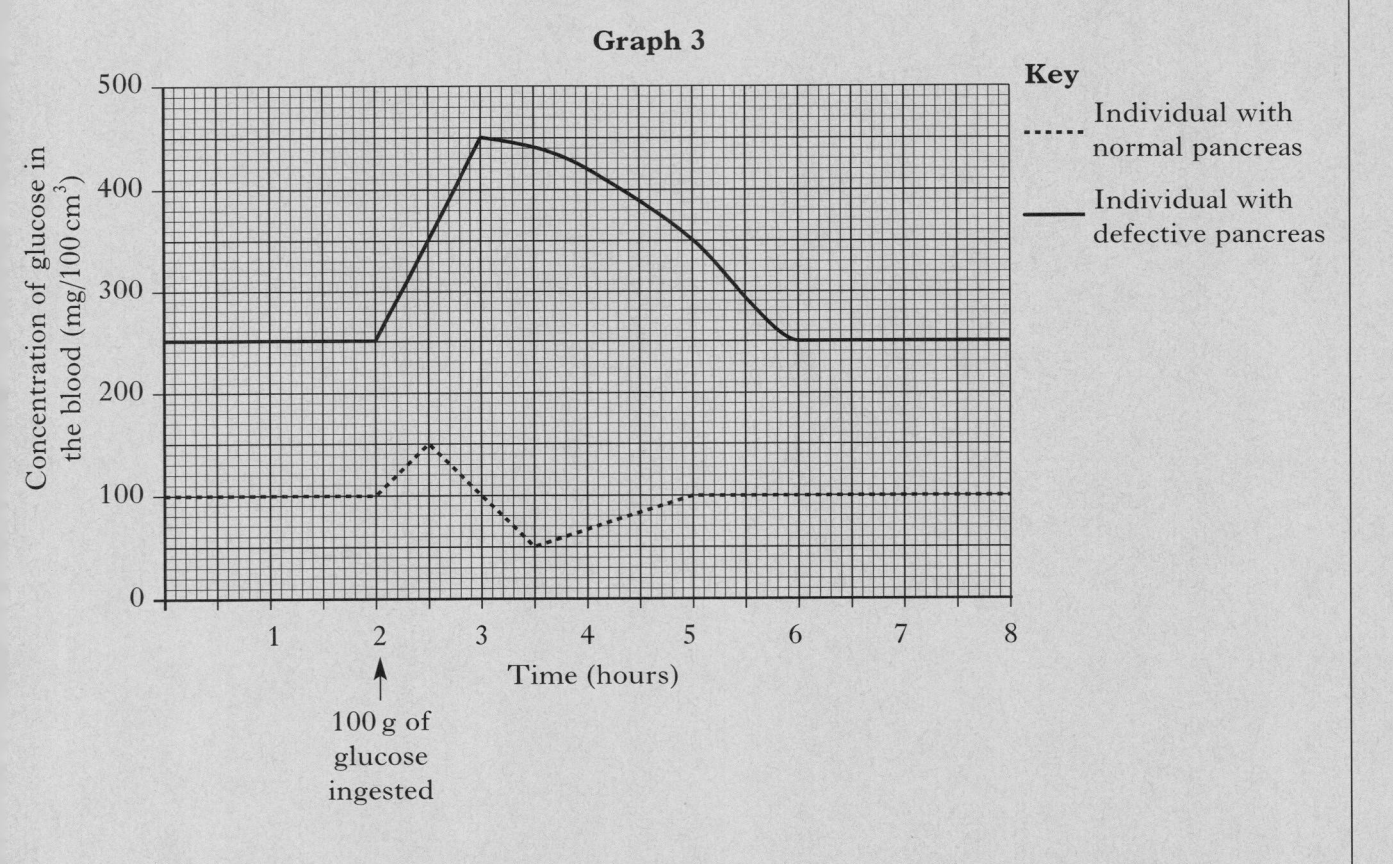

(f) From **Graph 3**, describe the changes in the blood glucose concentration of the individual with a normal pancreas after ingestion of 100 g of glucose.

_____

_____

_____   1

[Question 14 continues on *Page thirty-two*

14. (continued)

(g) From **Graph 3**, calculate the difference between the times taken for the concentration of glucose in the blood of the two individuals to return to a stable level from their maximum levels.

Space for calculation

Difference in time _____ **1**

(h) From **Graph 3** and **Graph 2**, calculate the concentration of insulin in the blood of the individual with the normal pancreas when their blood glucose level is stable.

Space for calculation

Concentration of insulin in the blood _____ units/cm^3 **1**

[Section C begins on *Page thirty-four*]

SPACE FOR ANSWERS

ADDITIONAL GRAPH PAPER FOR QUESTION 9(d)

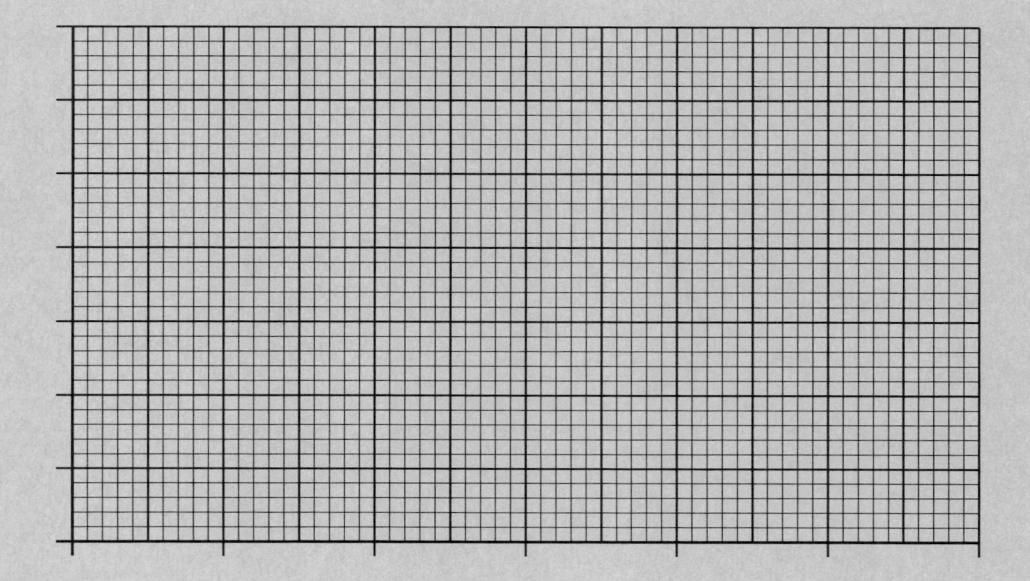

SECTION C

Both questions in this section should be attempted.

Note that each question contains a choice.

Questions 1 and 2 should be attempted on the blank pages which follow.

Supplementary sheets, if required, may be obtained from the invigilator.

Labelled diagrams may be used where appropriate.

Marks

1. Answer **either** A **or** B.

    A. Write notes on each of the following:

    (i) insulin production by genetic engineering; **6**

    (ii) the technique of somatic fusion in plants and one of its benefits. **4**

    (10)

    OR

    B. Write notes on each of the following:

    (i) foraging behaviour in animals; **4**

    (ii) social mechanisms in animals for obtaining food and for defence. **6**

    (10)

In question 2 ONE mark is available for coherence and ONE mark is available for relevance.

2. Answer **either** A **or** B.

    A. Give an account of *m*RNA synthesis and the role of *m*RNA in protein synthesis. **(10)**

    OR

    B. Give an account of the role of isolation mechanisms in the evolution of new species. **(10)**

[END OF QUESTION PAPER]

Official SQA Past Papers: Higher Biology 2001

FOR OFFICIAL USE

X007/301

NATIONAL QUALIFICATIONS 2001

MONDAY, 21 MAY 9.00 AM – 11.30 AM

BIOLOGY HIGHER

Total for Sections B and C

Fill in these boxes and read what is printed below.

Full name of centre

Town

Forename(s)

Surname

Date of birth
Day Month Year

Scottish candidate number

Number of seat

SECTION A—Questions 1–30 (30 marks)

Instructions for completion of Section A are given on page two.

SECTIONS B AND C (100 marks)

1. (a) All questions should be attempted.
   (b) It should be noted that in **Section C** questions 1 and 2 each contain a choice.
   (c) Question 4 is on pages 14, 15 and 16. Question 5 is on pages 17, 18 and 19. Pages 16 and 17 are fold-out pages. The additional graph paper is on page 37.

2. The questions may be answered in any order but all answers are to be written in the spaces provided in this answer book, and must be written clearly and legibly in ink.

3. Additional space for answers and rough work will be found at the end of the book. If further space is required, supplementary sheets may be obtained from the invigilator and should be inserted inside the **front** cover of this book.

4. The numbers of questions must be clearly inserted with any answers written in the additional space.

5. Rough work, if any should be necessary, should be written in this book and then scored through when the fair copy has been written.

6. Before leaving the examination room you must give this book to the invigilator. If you do not, you may lose all the marks for this paper.

SCOTTISH QUALIFICATIONS AUTHORITY

LIB X007/301 6/15270

SECTION A

Read carefully

1. Check that the answer sheet provided is for Biology Higher (Section A).
2. Fill in the details required on the answer sheet.
3. In this section a question is answered by indicating the choice A, B, C or D by a stroke made in **ink** in the appropriate place in the answer sheet—see the sample question below.
4. For each question there is only **one** correct answer.
5. Rough working, if required, should be done only on this question paper—or on the rough working sheet provided—**not** on the answer sheet.
6. At the end of the examination the answer sheet for Section A **must** be placed inside the front cover of this answer book.

Sample Question

The apparatus used to determine the energy stored in a foodstuff is a

A respirometer
B calorimeter
C klinostat
D gas burette.

The correct answer is **B**—calorimeter. A **heavy** vertical line should be drawn joining the two dots in the appropriate box in the column headed **B** as shown in the example on the answer sheet.

If, after you have recorded your answer, you decide that you have made an error and wish to make a change, you should cancel the original answer and put a vertical stroke in the box you now consider to be correct. Thus, if you want to change an answer D to an answer B, your answer sheet would look like this:

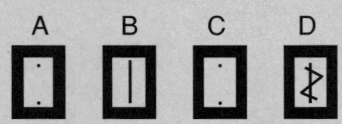

If you want to change back to an answer which has already been scored out, you should enter a tick (✓) to the **right** of the box of your choice, thus:

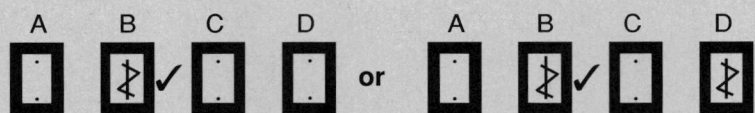

SECTION A

All questions in this section should be attempted.

Answers should be given on the separate answer sheet provided.

1. When an animal cell is immersed in a hypotonic solution it will

   A burst

   B become turgid

   C shrink

   D become flaccid.

2. Which statement referring to plant cell walls is correct?

   They contain

   A phospholipids and are permeable to solutes

   B carbohydrate and are permeable to solutes

   C phospholipids and are selectively permeable to solutes

   D carbohydrate and are selectively permeable to solutes.

3. Visking tubing is selectively permeable. In the experiment shown below to demonstrate osmosis, the following results were obtained.

   Initial mass of Visking
   tubing + contents   = 10·0 g

   Mass of Visking tubing + contents
   after experiment   = 8·2 g

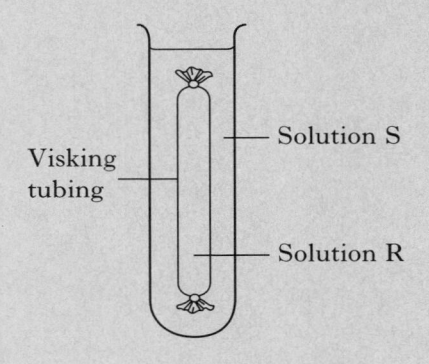

   The results shown would be obtained when

   A R is a 5% salt solution and S is a 10% salt solution

   B R is a 10% salt solution and S is a 5% salt solution

   C R is a 10% salt solution and S is water

   D R is a 5% salt solution and S is water.

4. The diagram below shows the energy flow in an area of forest canopy during 1 year.

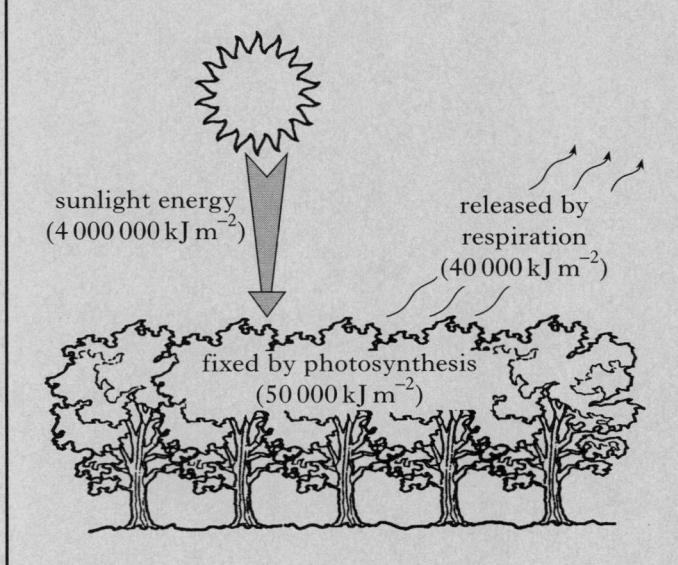

   sunlight energy ($4\,000\,000\,kJ\,m^{-2}$)

   released by respiration ($40\,000\,kJ\,m^{-2}$)

   fixed by photosynthesis ($50\,000\,kJ\,m^{-2}$)

   What percentages of available sunlight energy are fixed by the trees in photosynthesis and are present in new growth and stored food?

	Percentage of available energy fixed in photosynthesis	Percentage of available energy present in new growth and stored food
A	0·25	2·25
B	1·00	1·25
C	1·25	0·25
D	2·25	1·00

5. If a DNA molecule contains 8000 nucleotides of which 20% are adenine, then the number of guanine nucleotides present is

   A 1600

   B 2000

   C 2400

   D 3200.

   [Turn over

6. Which of the following is composed of protein?

A Antibody

B Glycogen

C Nucleotide

D Polysaccharide

7. The stages of infection of a host cell by a virus are listed below.

1 Host cell bursts, releasing new viruses.

2 Host cell DNA is inactivated.

3 Virus binds to host cell and injects DNA.

4 Virus DNA directs synthesis of new viruses.

The sequence in which these events occurs is

A 3,2,4,1

B 1,2,4,3

C 3,4,2,1

D 2,4,3,1.

8. Which of the following correctly identifies the functions of phagocytes and lymphocytes?

A Phagocytes produce antibodies; lymphocytes engulf bacteria.

B Phagocytes engulf bacteria; lymphocytes produce antibodies.

C Phagocytes produce antigens; lymphocytes produce antibodies.

D Phagocytes produce antibodies; lymphocytes produce antigens.

9. In tomato plants, the allele for purple stem **P** is dominant to its allele for green stem **p** and the allele for hairy stem **H** is dominant to its allele for smooth stem **h**. The following cross was carried out

PpHh × pphh

32 offspring were produced from this cross.

How many offspring would be expected to have purple, smooth stems?

A 24

B 16

C 8

D 4

10. A cross between two pea plants, one of which was heterozygous for seed colour and shape, produced offspring in the ratio of 3 with yellow, round seeds : 1 with yellow, wrinkled seeds.

What was the genotype of the other parent?

A Heterozygous for colour and shape

B Homozygous for seed colour only

C Homozygous for colour and shape

D Homozygous for seed shape only

Questions 11 and 12 refer to the information below.

The diagram shows the chromosome complement of cells during the development of abnormal sperm.

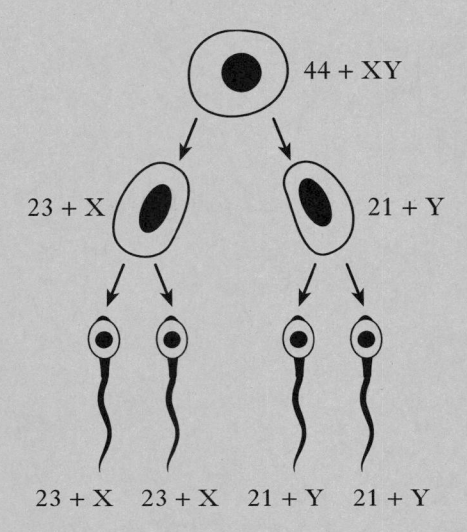

11. The diagram illustrates the effect of

A crossing over

B polygenic inheritance

C non-disjunction

D independent assortment of chromosomes.

12. A sperm with chromosome complement 23 + X fertilises a normal haploid egg. What is the chromosome number and sex of the resulting zygote?

	Chromosome number	Sex of zygote
A	24	female
B	46	female
C	46	male
D	47	female

13. The colour of tooth enamel is a sex-linked characteristic. The allele for brown tooth enamel (e) is recessive to the allele for normal tooth enamel (E). The following family tree refers to this condition.

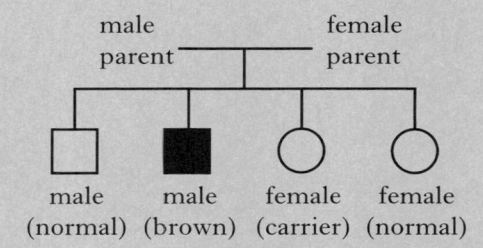

[Pedigree: male parent — female parent; children: male (normal), male (brown), female (carrier), female (normal)]

What are the genotypes of the parents?

A X^EY and X^EX^e
B X^EY and X^eX^e
C X^eY and X^EX^E
D X^eY and X^EX^e

14. Four genes, **P**, **R**, **S** and **T** are found on a pair of homologous chromosomes. Crosses were carried out and the cross-over value calculated, giving the following results.

Cross	Cross-over value
PpRr × pprr	32
PpSs × ppss	4
RrSs × rrss	28
RrTt × rrtt	10

Which of the following is the most likely sequence of genes on the chromosome?

A PTSR
B RSPT
C SPRT
D TRSP

15. The dark variety of the peppered moth became common in industrial areas of Britain following the increase in the production of soot during the Industrial Revolution.

The increase in the dark form was due to

A dark moths migrating to areas which gave the best camouflage
B a change in the prey species taken by birds
C an increase in the mutation rate
D a change in selection pressure.

16. A new species of organism is considered to have evolved when a population

A is isolated from the rest of the population by a geographical barrier
B shows increased variation due to mutations
C can no longer interbreed with the rest of the population
D is subjected to increased selection pressures in its habitat.

17. Reproductive incompatibility between different species of plant may be overcome by

A recombinant DNA technology
B the use of mutagens
C somatic fusion of cells
D using polyploid parents.

18. The table shows the effect of the water content of the guard cells on the state of a stoma. Which line is correct?

	stoma open/closed	state of guard cells
A	open	flaccid
B	open	plasmolysed
C	closed	flaccid
D	closed	turgid

[Turn over

19. Which of the following are adaptations of xerophytic plants?

   A Leaves with small surface area and a thin waxy cuticle

   B Leaves which are rolled and covered in hairs

   C Leaves with a large surface area and a thick waxy cuticle

   D Leaves which are hairy and have many stomata

20. Grass is a plant which can survive despite being grazed constantly by herbivores such as sheep and cattle. It is able to tolerate grazing because

   A it is a wind-pollinated plant

   B it grows constantly throughout the year

   C it possesses poisons which protect it from being eaten entirely

   D it has very low growing points which send up new leaves when older ones are eaten.

21. Phenylketonuria is a condition that results from

   A differential gene expression

   B chromosome non-disjunction

   C the influence of an environmental factor

   D an inherited gene mutation.

22. The plant growth substance IAA (indole acetic acid) is of benefit to humans because it can function

   A as a herbicide and as a rooting powder

   B as a herbicide and to break dormancy

   C in the malting of barley and to break dormancy

   D as a rooting powder and in the malting of barley.

23. An investigation was carried out into the effect of IAA concentration on the growth of shoots of two species of plant. The graph below gives a summary of the results.

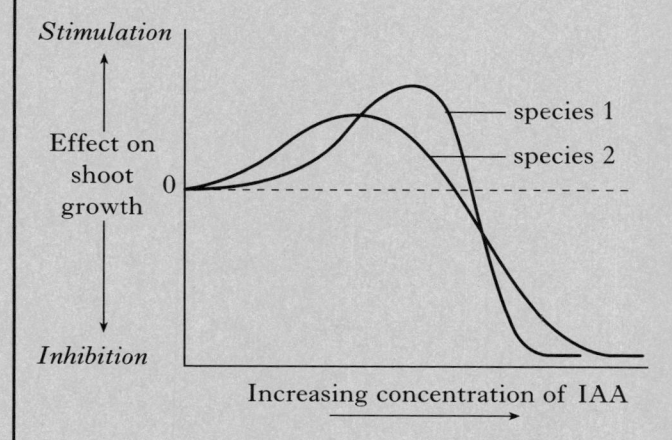

Which one of the following conclusions is justified?

   A Species 1 shows its maximum stimulation at a lower IAA concentration than species 2

   B Species 2 is more inhibited by the highest concentrations of IAA than species 1

   C Species 2 is stimulated over a greater range of IAA concentrations than species 1

   D Species 1 is stimulated by some IAA concentrations which inhibit species 2

24. Which of the following developments, in the growth of a flowering plant, is caused by gibberellic acid (GA)?

   A Growth of dwarf plants to normal heights

   B Breakdown of cellulose by barley embryos

   C Leaf abscission

   D Stimulation of fruit formation

25. Plants grown in the dark have

   A green leaves and short internodes

   B green leaves and long internodes

   C yellow leaves and short internodes

   D yellow leaves and long internodes.

26. The graph shows the changes in concentration of starch and of a red pigment, lycopene, which occur as tomatoes ripen.

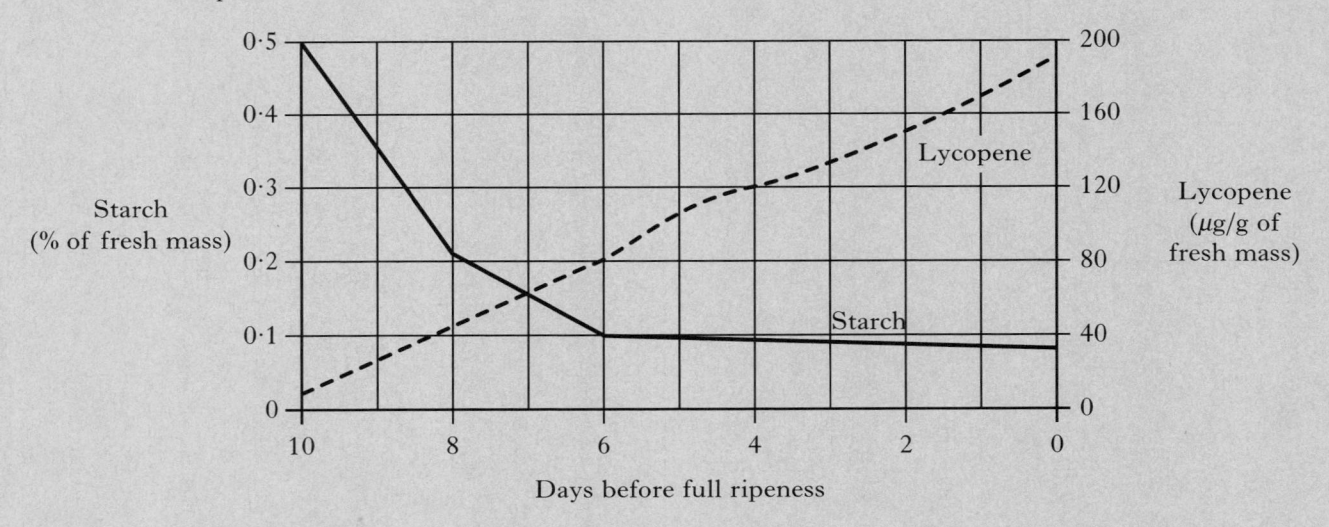

What valid conclusion may be made from the graph?

During the ripening process of tomatoes,

A starch is converted into the red pigment lycopene

B starch is broken down and lycopene is synthesised

C starch is broken down to provide energy for the synthesis of lycopene

D the faster starch is broken down, the greater the rate of synthesis of lycopene.

27. Which line identifies correctly the effect of increased secretion of Anti Diuretic hormone (ADH) on the composition and volume of urine?

	Concentration of urea	Concentration of glucose	Volume of urine
A	no change	no change	increase
B	increase	increase	decrease
C	increase	no change	decrease
D	decrease	no change	increase

28. Which of the following correctly identifies the locations of the centres that monitor blood water concentration and temperature in humans?

	Blood water concentration	Temperature
A	Hypothalamus	Pituitary gland
B	Hypothalamus	Hypothalamus
C	Pituitary gland	Hypothalamus
D	Pituitary gland	Pituitary gland

[Turn over

29. Which of the following graphs correctly shows the relationship between prey and predator populations?

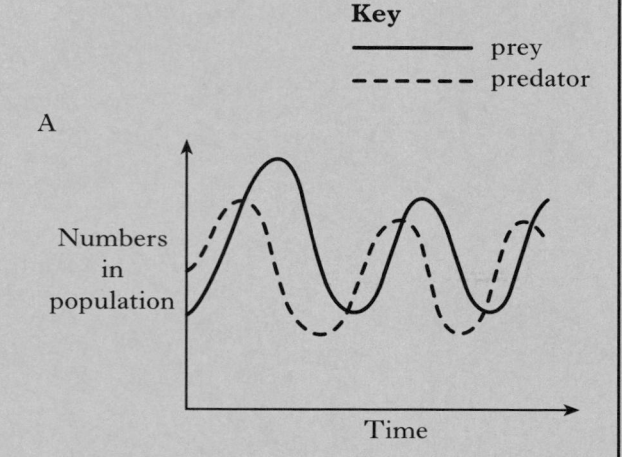

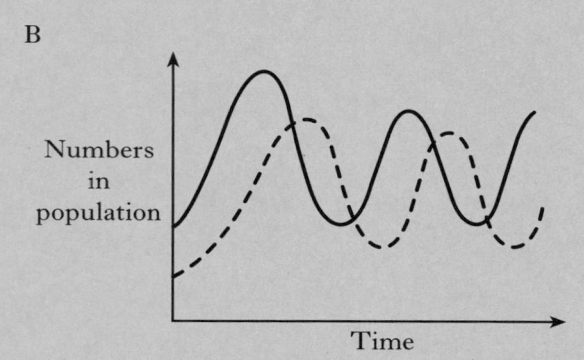

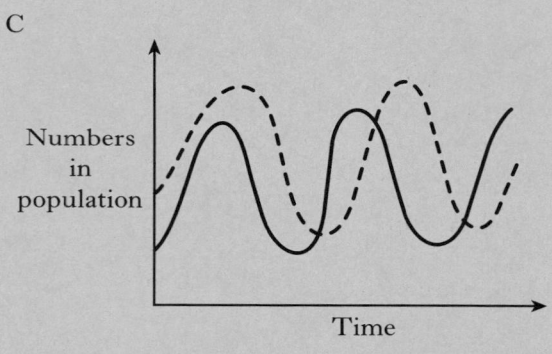

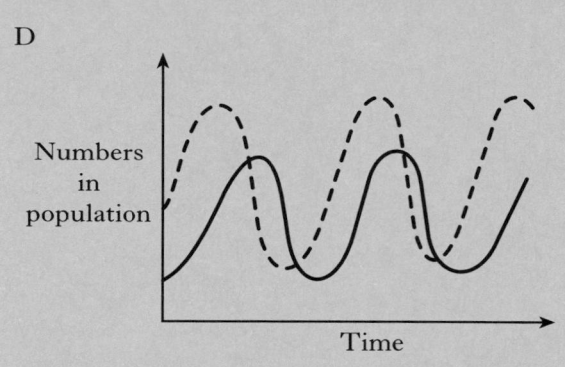

Key
— prey
----- predator

A, B, C, D: graphs of Numbers in population vs Time

30. List P gives three reasons why population monitoring may be carried out.

List Q gives three species that are monitored by scientists.

List P	List Q
1 Valuable food resource	W Stonefly
2 Endangered species	X Humpback whale
3 Indicator species	Y Haddock

Which of the following correctly matches reasons from list P with organisms from list Q?

	Reasons		
	1	2	3
A	W	X	Y
B	Y	W	X
C	X	Y	W
D	Y	X	W

[Turn over for Section B on *Page ten*]

DO NOT WRITE IN THIS MARGIN

Marks

SECTION B

All questions in this section should be attempted.

1. (*a*) The graph below shows the absorption spectra for the leaf pigments extracted from two species of woodland plant.

Species X is a sun plant.

Species Y is a shade plant.

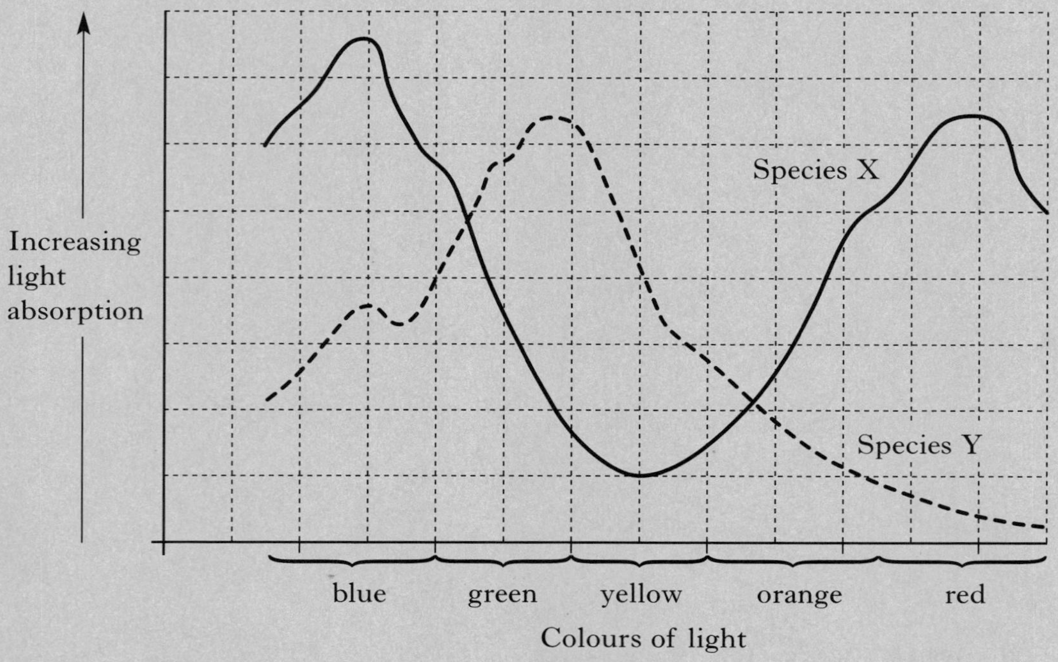

Increasing light absorption
Species X
Species Y
blue
green
yellow
orange
red
Colours of light

(i) Which colour of light would be most strongly reflected by the pigments in Species X?

______________________________ **1**

(ii) Apart from being absorbed or reflected, what else can happen to light which strikes the pigments in a leaf?

______________________________ **1**

(iii) Explain how the absorption spectrum of Species Y shows that it is well adapted for growth in the shade of Species X.

____

____

______________________________ **2**

1. (continued)

(b) The diagram below shows a summary of the light stage of photosynthesis.

```
[Light energy absorbed    →    [Hydrogen and ATP produced
 by pigments]                    for use in the Calvin cycle]
```

(i) Describe how hydrogen is produced in the light stage of photosynthesis.

_____

_____ 1

(ii) Name the substance that transfers hydrogen to the Calvin cycle.

Name _____ 1

(c) Complete the diagram of the Calvin Cycle below by inserting the appropriate letter from the table into each box.

Process	Letter
Carbon dioxide combines with RuBP	P
Glucose formed	Q
GP formed	R

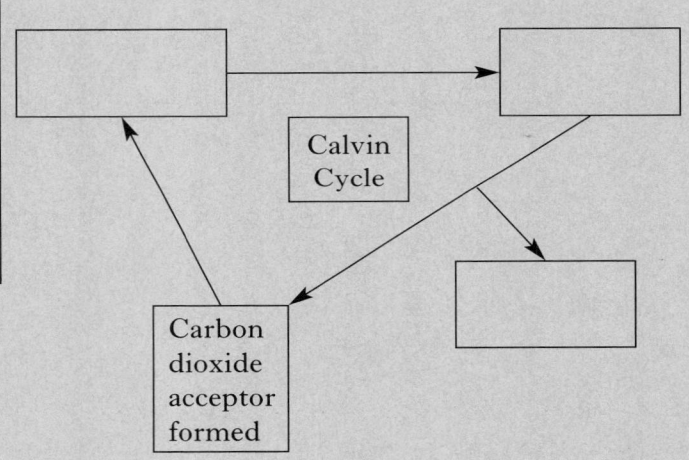

1

[Turn over

2. The diagram below shows the arrangement of molecules in part of a cell membrane.

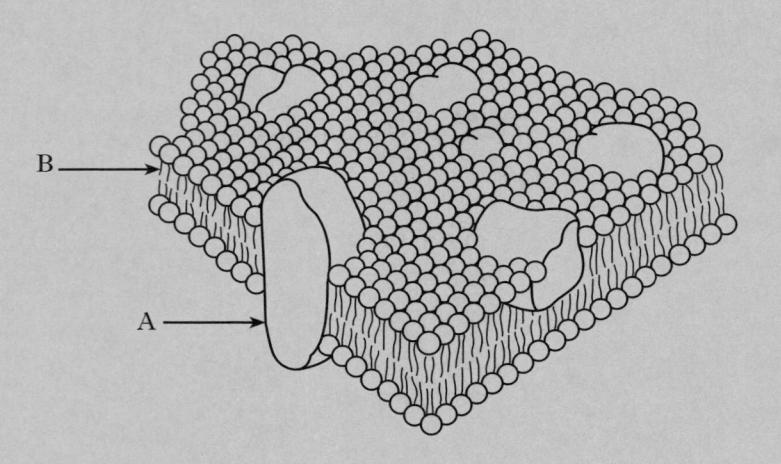

(a) Name the molecules represented by A and B.

A _____

B _____   1

(b) Many structures in a cell are made of membranes. The grid below shows the names of some of these structures.

1 cristae	2 endoplasmic reticulum	3 Golgi apparatus
4 nuclear membrane	5 grana	6 lysosome

(i) From the grid, select the structure that fits each of the following descriptions.

Description   *Structure*

Contains photosynthetic pigments   _____

Ribosomes are attached to the outer surface   _____   1

(ii) From the grid, select the structure involved in phagocytosis and describe its function in this process.

Structure _____

Function _____

_____   1

3. (a) The diagram below shows the pathway of anaerobic respiration in human muscle tissue.

Glucose □

↓ Process X

Pyruvic acid □

↓

Compound S   3C

(i) Name Process X and Compound S.

Process X _____   Compound S _____

(ii) Complete the boxes in the diagram to show the number of carbon atoms present in glucose and pyruvic acid.

(iii) Aerobic respiration in human muscle tissue involves the Krebs cycle and the cytochrome system.

For each statement in the table below, tick (✓) a box to show the process to which it applies.

Statement	Krebs cycle	Cytochrome system
Carbon dioxide is produced		
Occurs on the cristae of the mitochondria		
Involves the formation of NADH$_2$		
Involves the formation of citric acid		

(b) The diagram below shows the synthesis and breakdown of ATP.

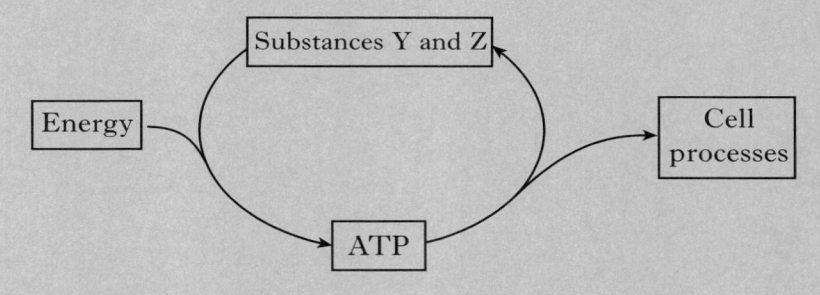

Energy → [Substances Y and Z] → ATP → Cell processes → (back to Substances Y and Z)

(i) Name substances Y and Z.

Substance Y _____   Substance Z _____

(ii) Give an example of a process in muscle cells which requires energy from ATP.

_____

_____

4. The effect of temperature on the rate of respiration in yeast was measured by the time taken for the yeast to decolourise a chemical called resazurin.

The method used in the investigation is outlined below.

1. A suspension of yeast cells in water was prepared two days before the experiment.

2. Water baths were set up at a range of temperatures.

3. Three test tubes were placed in each water bath.
   - Test tube 1 contained 10 cm³ of blue resazurin solution
   - Test tube 2 contained 10 cm³ of glucose solution
   - Test tube 3 contained 10 cm³ of yeast suspension

4. When the contents of the test tubes reached the required temperature, they were mixed thoroughly together in a separate test tube. The test tube containing the mixture was then returned to the appropriate water bath.

5. The time taken for the resazurin to become colourless at each temperature was noted.

The results are shown in the table below.

Temperature (°C)	Time for resazurin to become colourless (seconds)
15	360
20	240
25	180
30	120
35	90
40	60
45	180

(a) What evidence from the results supports the statement that respiration is an enzyme controlled process?

[Question 4 continues on *Page fifteen* and fold-out *Page sixteen*

4. (continued)

(b) Other test tubes should be set up at each temperature to act as controls. Complete the table below to show the contents of **two** such controls and their purpose in the investigation.

Contents of controls	Purpose in the investigation
10 cm³ of blue resazurin solution 10 cm³ of glucose solution 10 cm³ of dead yeast in suspension	
	To show that all storage carbohydrate was used up before yeast suspension was used in the experiments

2

(c) The resazurin solution, glucose solution and yeast suspension must be kept separate in the water bath until the contents have reached the experimental temperature. If this had not been done, how would the results in the water bath at 40 °C have differed from the results obtained? Explain your answer.

Difference _____

Explanation _____

_____

_____

1

[Question 4 continues on *Page sixteen*

4. **(continued)**

   (d) On the grid below plot a line graph of time for resazurin to become colourless against temperature.

   (Additional graph paper, if required, can be found on page 37.)

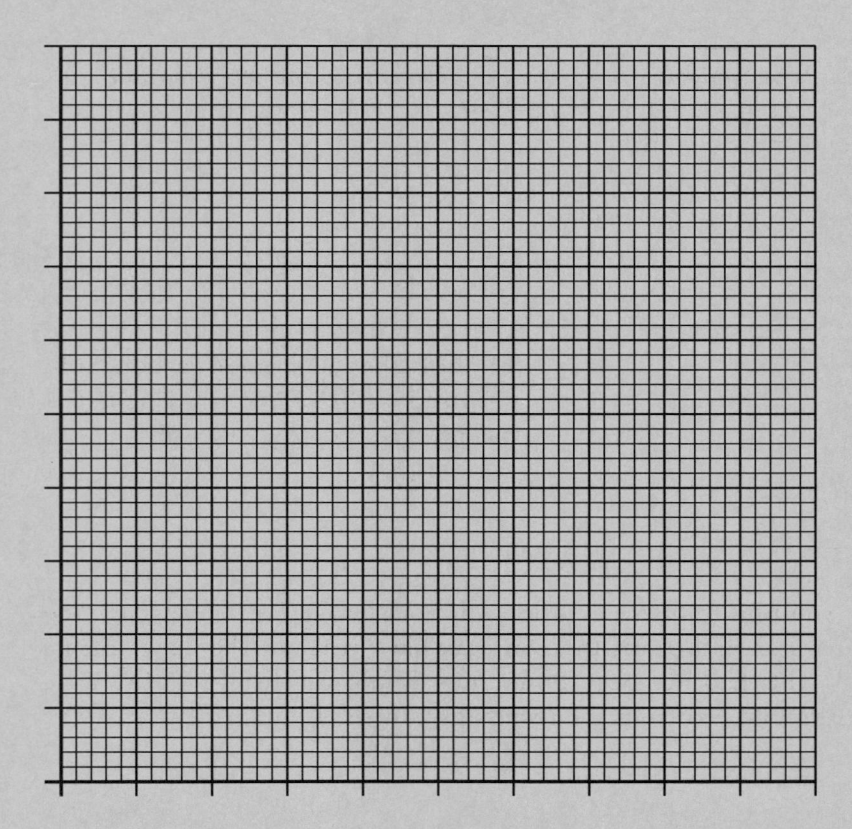

   2

   (e) Identify **two** variables which must be kept the same at each temperature in order to make the results obtained valid.

   1 _____

   2 _____   1

   [Question 5 begins on fold-out *Page seventeen*]

5. (a) The diagram below shows some of the processes which take place during synthesis of protein in a cell.

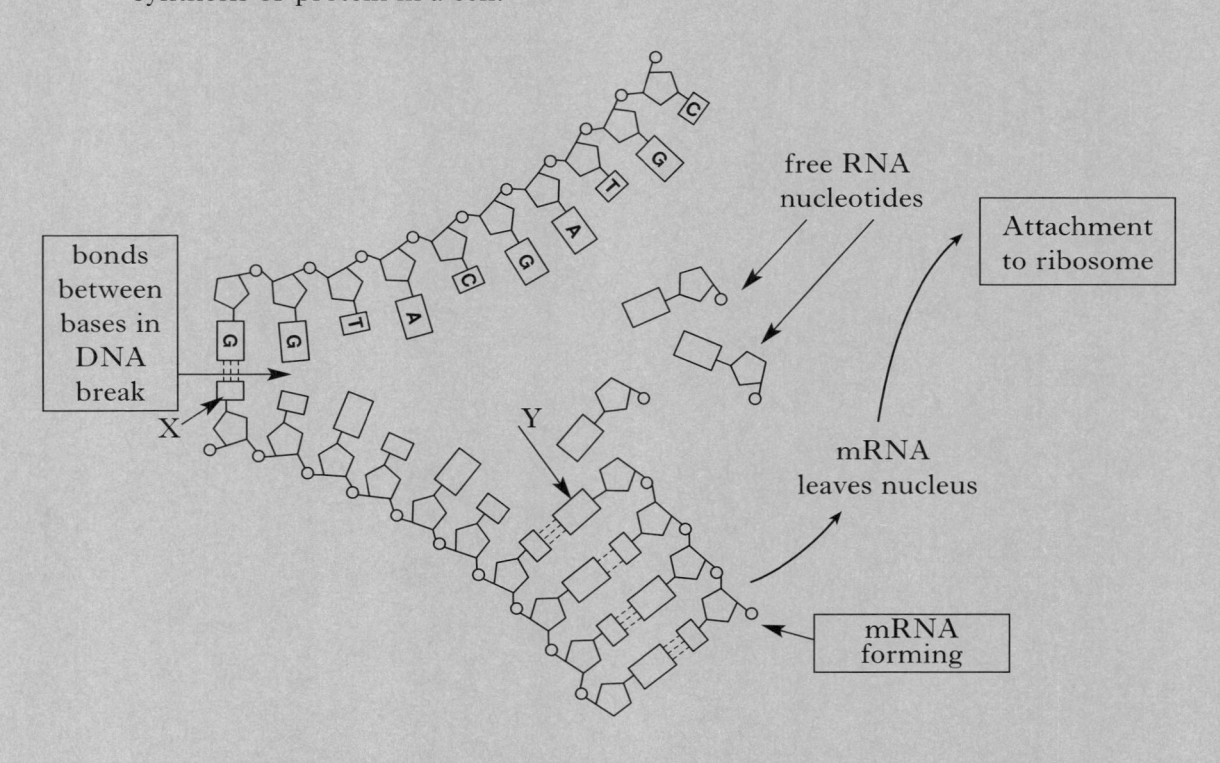

(i) Name the type of bond that holds pairs of bases in DNA together.

_____

(ii) Name **two** substances present in RNA which are **not** present in DNA.

1 _____

2 _____

(iii) Name bases X and Y.

Base X _____

Base Y _____

(iv) Name the bond that links amino acids together.

_____

5. **(a) (continued)**

(v) The diagram below shows the amino acids in part of a protein molecule.

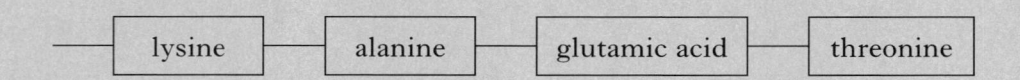

— lysine — alanine — glutamic acid — threonine —

The table shows the mRNA codons for the amino acids shown in the diagram.

Amino acid	Codon
Alanine	GCC
Glutamic acid	GAA
Lysine	AAG
Threonine	ACU

Write the sequence of bases in the DNA that would code for the sequence of amino acids shown in the diagram.

Space for working

Answer _____ 1

(vi) Describe the roles of tRNA in protein synthesis.

_____

_____

_____ 2

(b) Sickle cell anaemia is a genetically transmitted disorder which causes abnormal haemoglobin to be formed.

The amino acid sequence of part of a haemoglobin molecule and the same part of an abnormal haemoglobin molecule are shown below.

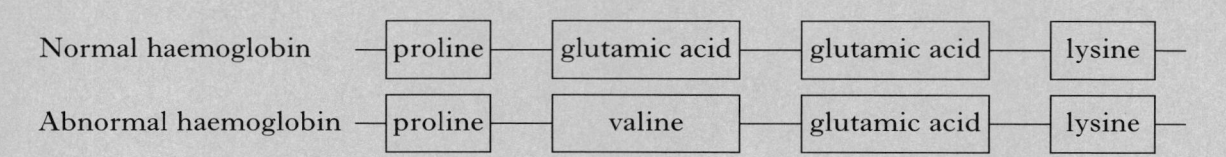

Normal haemoglobin — proline — glutamic acid — glutamic acid — lysine —

Abnormal haemoglobin — proline — valine — glutamic acid — lysine —

Describe the difference between the two forms of haemoglobin and name a type of gene mutation which would cause this effect.

Difference _____

Type of gene mutation _____ 1

5. **(continued)**

(c) The family-tree below shows the inheritance of sickle cell anaemia over four generations. The allele for normal haemoglobin (**H**) is dominant to the allele for abnormal haemoglobin (**h**).

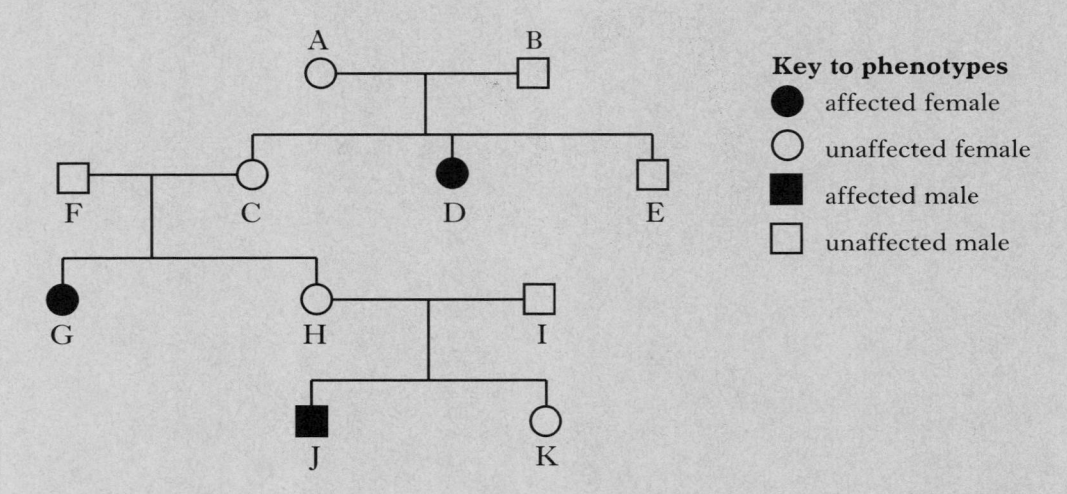

Key to phenotypes
- ● affected female
- ○ unaffected female
- ■ affected male
- □ unaffected male

(i) From the family-tree, explain why individuals F and C can both be identified as being heterozygous for the condition.

_____

_____

_____

(ii) What is the chance that individual K is heterozygous for the condition?
Space for working

Chance _____

[Turn over

6. (a) The diagram below represents an early stage in the process of meiosis in a cell from the testes of an insect.

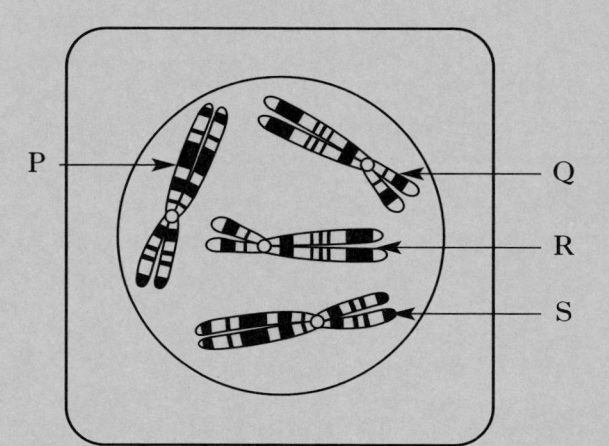

Which letter shows the homologous partner of chromosome P?

Letter _____

(b) The diagrams below show five later stages in the process of meiosis. The diagrams are **not** in the correct order.

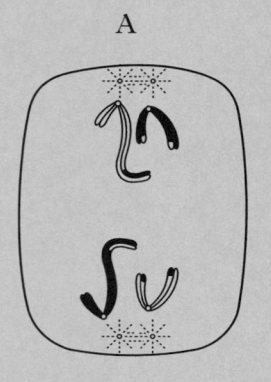

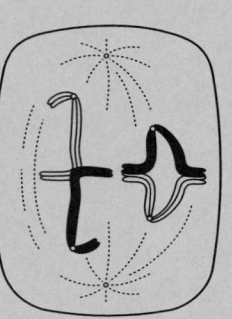

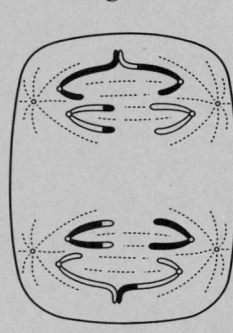

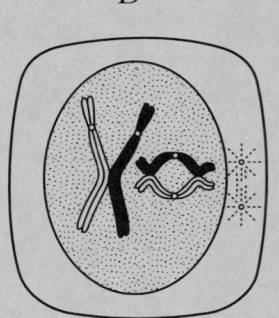

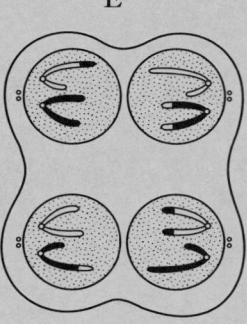

Using the letters, show the order in which these stages occur during the process of meiosis.

_____ → _____ → _____ → _____ → _____

6. (continued)

   (c) Apart from mutations, state **two** other events which occur during meiosis that result in genetic variation.

   1 _____

   2 _____   2

[Turn over

7. The diagram below represents the evolution of one species of modern wheat (*Triticum vulgare*) through polyploidy.

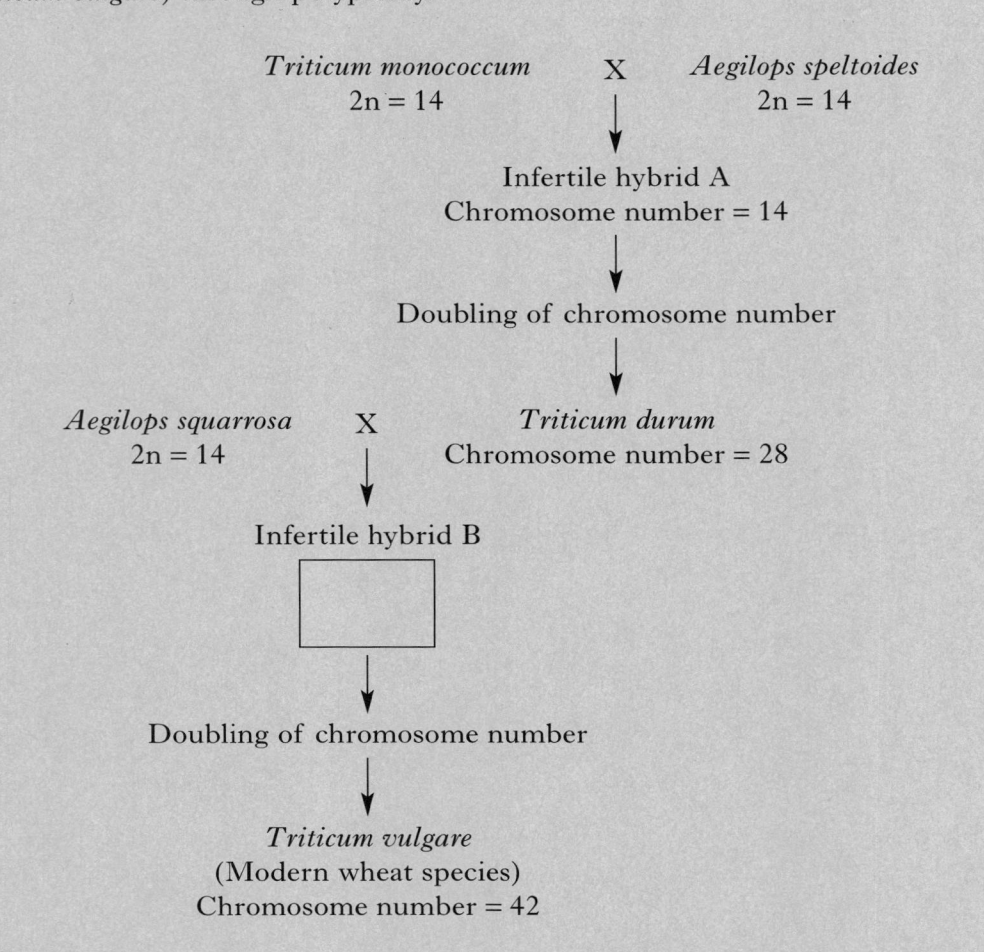

Triticum monococcum   X   *Aegilops speltoides*
2n = 14   2n = 14

↓

Infertile hybrid A
Chromosome number = 14

↓

Doubling of chromosome number

↓

Aegilops squarrosa   X   *Triticum durum*
2n = 14   Chromosome number = 28

↓

Infertile hybrid B

↓

Doubling of chromosome number

↓

Triticum vulgare
(Modern wheat species)
Chromosome number = 42

(a) Write the chromosome number of infertile hybrid B into the box in the diagram. **1**

(b) By how many times is the haploid number of modern wheat greater than that of the earliest wheat *Triticum monococcum*?

Space for calculation

Number of times _____ **1**

(c) Name the **two** species in the diagram which can be described as being polyploid.

1 _____   2 _____ **1**

7. (continued)

(d) Give **one** advantage for humans of polyploidy in crop plants such as wheat.

(e) Why is it important to conserve species of *Triticum* such as *Triticum durum* and *Triticum monococcum*?

8. (a) The Galapagos islands are an isolated group of islands that lie 1500 kilometres from the mainland of South America.

It is believed that at one time in the past, members of a species of finch were blown across to the islands and evolved in isolation.

There are now 14 species of finch on the islands. Each species exploits a different food source. This can best be seen from the shapes of their beaks.

The diagrams below show the beaks of three different species of finch on the islands.

(i) Explain how the evolution of these species of finch illustrates adaptive radiation.

_____

_____

_____ 2

(ii) Name **two** isolation mechanisms involved in the evolution of new species.

1 _____

2 _____ 1

8. (continued)

(b) The table below shows the mass of water gained and lost by a desert rat over a 24 hour period.

	Mass of water lost or gained (g)
Food	6
Metabolic water	54
Exhalation	45
Urine	12
Faeces	3

(i) What evidence from the table supports the statement that homeostatic control of water occurs in desert rats?

_____

_____ 1

(ii) Describe **one** behavioural adaptation shown by the desert rat to reduce water loss and explain how this helps in water conservation.

Adaptation _____

Explanation _____

_____ 1

[Turn over

9. (a) A species of marine worm responds to sudden decreases in light intensity by withdrawing into its tube.

In an experiment, 20 worms were exposed to the stimulus at 1 minute intervals for 6 minutes.

Trial number	Number of worms showing a response
1	20
2	20
3	16
4	10
5	4
6	0

(i) Complete the table below by inserting the type of behaviour shown at trials 1 and 6.

Trial number	Type of behaviour
1	
6	

(ii) What is the advantage to the marine worms of the change in behaviour that occurs between trials 1 and 6?

_____

_____

9. **(continued)**

(b) Hawks are predators which attack flocks of pigeons. The table shows how the percentage of attack success of a predatory hawk varies with the number of pigeons in the flock.

Number of pigeons in the flock	% attack success
2	80
10	50
20	40
40	15

Suggest an explanation for the effect of flock size on attack success shown in the table.

_____

_____

(c) Some hawk species show cooperative hunting behaviour.
Explain **one** advantage of this type of behaviour.

_____

_____

[Turn over

10. (a) The diagram below represents the appearance of some of the cells in a plant root.

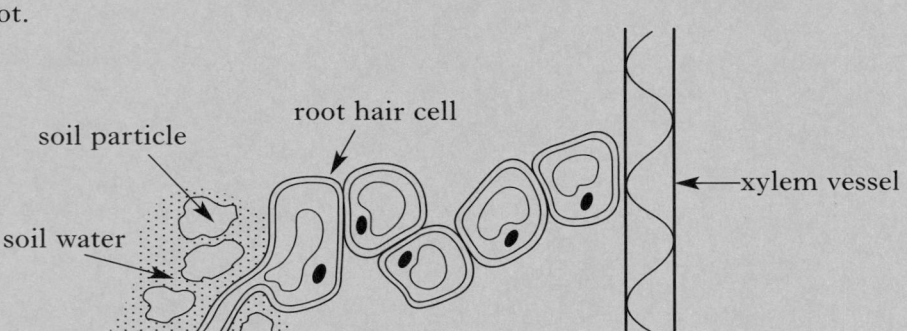

(i) Explain how water moves from the soil into the root hair cell.

(ii) Name the two forces which allow water to rise as a continuous column within the xylem vessel.

1 _____ 2 _____

(b) The diagram below shows two transverse sections of a stem taken from the same branch.

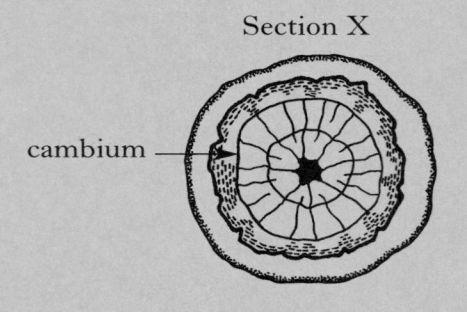

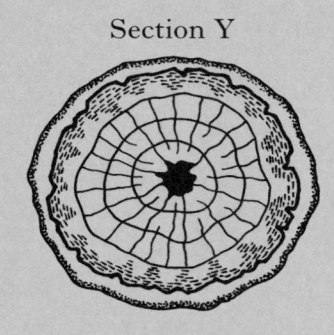

(i) State the number of annual rings present in each section.

Section X _____ Section Y _____

(ii) State the role of cambium in the formation of annual rings.

(iii) Describe **one** way in which the structure of a spring xylem vessel differs from that of a summer xylem vessel.

10. (continued)

(c) Leaves of the same surface area from the same shrub were treated as shown in **Diagram 1** below. The results after 1 hour, in conditions that promoted water loss, are shown in **Diagram 2**.

Diagram 1
(Mass of leaves balanced)

Leaf A — Lower surface coated with vaseline
Leaf B — Upper surface coated with vaseline

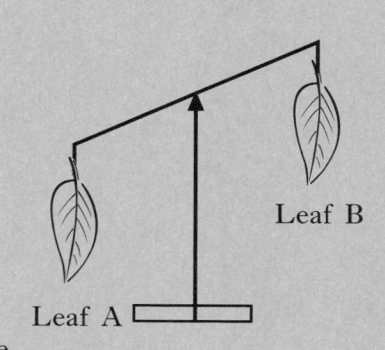

Diagram 2

Leaf A
Leaf B

(i) In the following sentences, **underline** one of the alternatives in each pair to make the sentences correct.

The leaf which has {more / fewer} stomata exposed will lose more mass.

This is {leaf A / leaf B} which shows that more stomata are present on

the {upper / lower} leaf surface.

(ii) Name a factor that affects the rate of transpiration.
Explain how changes in this factor can cause a decrease in the rate of transpiration.

Factor _____

Explanation _____

_____

[Turn over

11. The diagrams below represent the same barley seedling at 24 hours and 30 hours after germination.

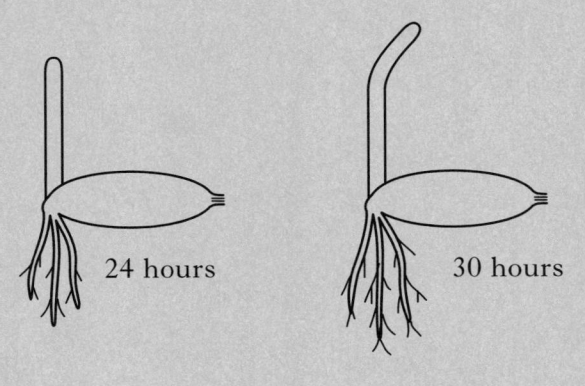

24 hours   30 hours

(a) Describe the environmental condition which would result in the direction of shoot growth shown at 30 hours.

_____

_____ 1

(b) Gibberellic acid (GA) has a role in the germination of barley grains.

(i) Name the part of the barley grain that produces GA.

Name _____ 1

(ii) GA causes part of the barley grain to produce an enzyme. Name the part of the grain and the enzyme produced.

Part of barley grain _____

Enzyme _____ 1

(c) Describe the role of Indole Acetic Acid (IAA) in apical dominance.

_____

_____ 1

12. Flower production in plants may be controlled by the photoperiod.

(a) Explain what is meant by "photoperiod."

_____

_____

(b) In an experiment, four plants of the same species were exposed to repeated cycles of light and dark. The flowering responses are shown in the table below.

Plant	Light period (hours)	Dark period (hours)	Flowering response of plant
1	13	11	Flowers produced
2	14	10	No flowers produced
3	12	12	Flowers produced
4	15	9	No flowers produced

Using information from the table, complete the sentence below.

In order for plants of this species to flower, they require a minimum _____ period of _____ hours.

13. An investigation was carried out into the uptake of potassium ions by animal cells.

Graph 1 shows the rates of potassium ion uptake and breakdown of glucose at 30 °C in solutions with different concentrations of oxygen.

Graph 2 shows the effect of temperature on the rate of uptake of potassium ions at a constant oxygen concentration.

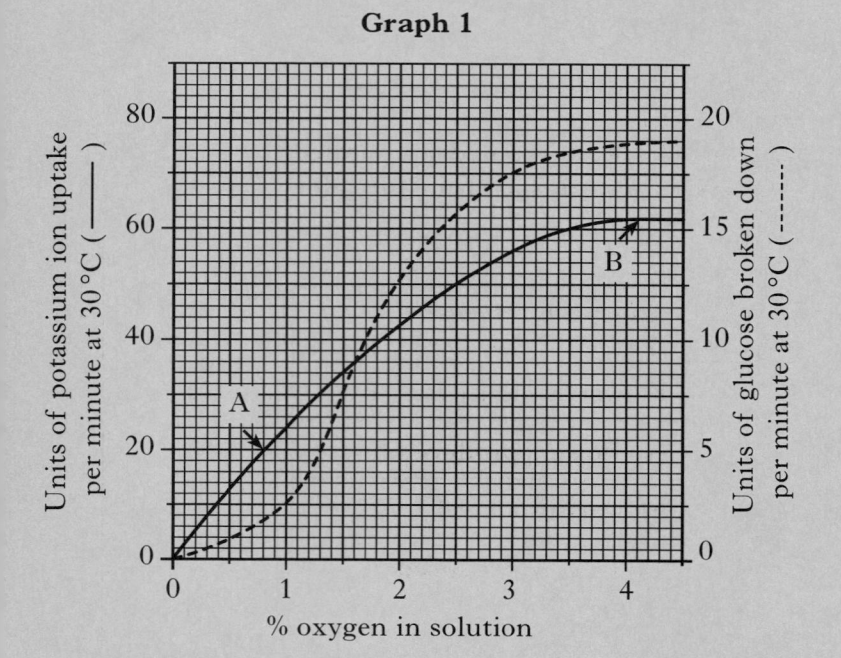

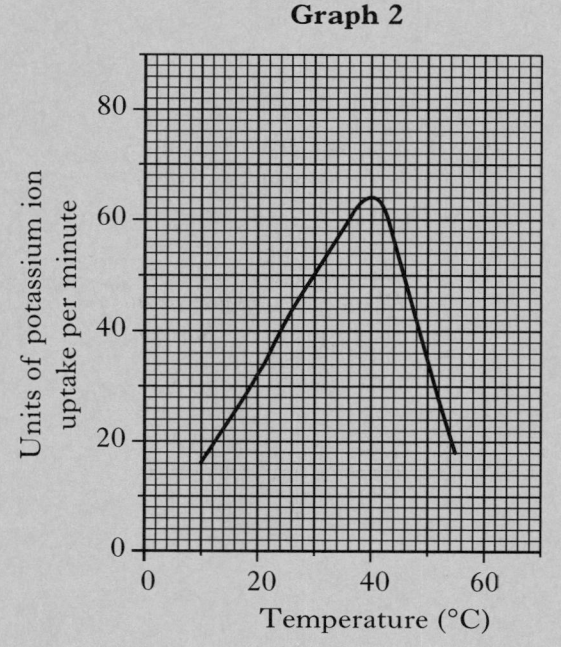

(a) From **Graph 1**, calculate the percentage increase in the rate of glucose breakdown when the concentration of oxygen in solution is increased from 1·0% to 1·5%.

Space for calculation

Percentage _____ %

(b) From **Graph 1**, explain the effect of increasing oxygen concentration on the rate of potassium ion uptake.

13. (continued)

(c) From the information in **Graphs 1** and **2**, find the oxygen concentration at which the results shown in **Graph 2** were obtained.

Space for calculation

% oxygen in solution _____ **1**

(d) (i) What evidence from **Graph 1** supports the statement that the percentage of oxygen in solution is limiting potassium ion uptake at point A?

_____

_____ **1**

(ii) Name a factor that could be limiting potassium ion uptake at point B on **Graph 1**.

Factor _____ **1**

(e) Express, as the **simplest whole number ratio**, the units of potassium ion uptake per minute at 10 °C, 20 °C and 40 °C.

Space for calculation

Ratio _____ : _____ : _____ **1**

[Turn over

14. (a) The flow chart below represents part of the homeostatic control of blood glucose concentration in a human.

```
              Normal blood glucose
                 concentration
          ┌────────────┴────────────┐
          ▼                         ▼
  Increased blood glucose    Decreased blood glucose
  concentration detected     concentration detected
     by receptor cells          by receptor cells
          │                         │
          ▼                         ▼
  Increased secretion of     Decreased secretion of
       hormone X                   hormone X
  Decreased secretion of     Increased secretion of
       hormone Y                   hormone Y
          │                         │
          └──────────┬──────────────┘
                     ▼
              Normal blood glucose
                 concentration
```

(i) Name the organ that contains the receptor cells.

Name _____   1

(ii) Name hormones X and Y.

Hormone X _____

Hormone Y _____   1

(iii) Excess glucose is converted to a storage carbohydrate within a body organ. Name the storage carbohydrate and the body organ within which it is stored.

Carbohydrate _____

Organ _____   1

14. (continued)

(b) The list below contains terms used to illustrate the control of lactose metabolism in the bacterium *Escherichia coli*.

List of terms
Structural gene
Repressor molecule
Inducer
Operator
Regulator gene
Lactose

Which term matches each of the following descriptions?

Description	Term
Produces repressor protein.	_____
Combines with lactose.	_____
Produces the lactose digesting enzyme.	_____
Acts as the inducer.	_____

3

[Turn over for Section C on *Page thirty-six*

SECTION C

Both questions in this section should be attempted.

Note that each question contains a choice.

Questions 1 and 2 should be attempted on the blank pages which follow.

Supplementary sheets, if required, may be obtained from the invigilator.

Labelled diagrams may be used where appropriate.

Marks

1. Answer **either** A **or** B.

    A. Write notes on each of the following:

    (i) succession and climax in plant communities; **5**

    (ii) the influence of density-dependent factors on population changes. **5**

    (10)

    OR

    B. Write notes on each of the following:

    (i) the importance of nitrogen and magnesium in plant growth and development and symptoms of their deficiency; **6**

    (ii) the importance of vitamin D and iron in humans. **4**

    (10)

In question 2, ONE mark is available for coherence and ONE mark is available for relevance.

2. Answer **either** A **or** B.

    A. Give an account of production of protein by genetic engineering and state the advantages of this technique. **(10)**

    OR

    B. Give an account of the osmotic problems of salt water bony fish and describe how water balance is maintained in such fish. **(10)**

[END OF QUESTION PAPER]

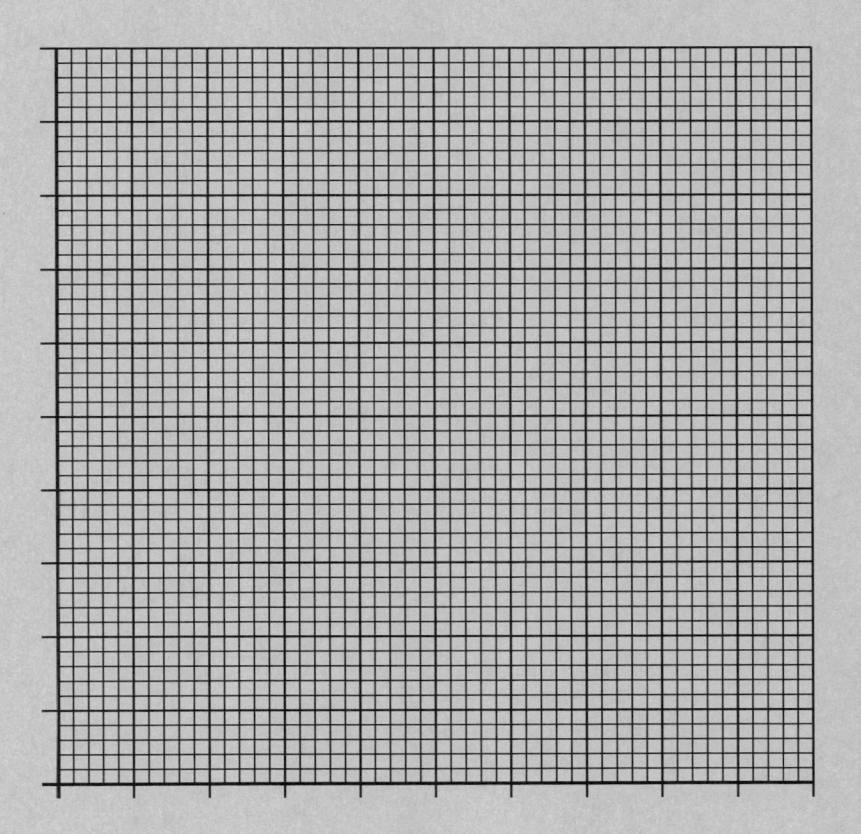

SPACE FOR ANSWERS

ADDITIONAL GRAPH PAPER FOR QUESTION 4(*d*)

SPACE FOR ANSWERS

Official SQA Past Papers: Higher Biology 2002

FOR OFFICIAL USE

Total for Sections B and C

X007/301

NATIONAL QUALIFICATIONS 2002

FRIDAY, 31 MAY 1.00 PM – 3.30 PM

BIOLOGY HIGHER

Fill in these boxes and read what is printed below.

Full name of centre

Town

Forename(s)

Surname

Date of birth
Day Month Year

Scottish candidate number

Number of seat

SECTION A—Questions 1–30 (30 marks)

Instructions for completion of Section A are given on page two.

SECTIONS B AND C (100 marks)

1 (a) All questions should be attempted.

   (b) It should be noted that in **Section C** questions 1 and 2 each contain a choice.

   (c) Question 9 is on pages 22, 23 and 24. Question 10 is on pages 25, 26 and 27. Pages 24 and 25 are fold-out pages. The additional graph paper is on page 36.

2 The questions may be answered in any order but all answers are to be written in the spaces provided in this answer book, and must be written clearly and legibly in ink.

3 Additional space for answers and rough work will be found at the end of the book. If further space is required, supplementary sheets may be obtained from the invigilator and should be inserted inside the **front** cover of this book.

4 The numbers of questions must be clearly inserted with any answers written in the additional space.

5 Rough work, if any should be necessary, should be written in this book and then scored through when the fair copy has been written.

6 Before leaving the examination room you must give this book to the invigilator. If you do not, you may lose all the marks for this paper.

SCOTTISH QUALIFICATIONS AUTHORITY

SECTION A

Read carefully

1. Check that the answer sheet provided is for Biology Higher (Section A).
2. Fill in the details required on the answer sheet.
3. In this section a question is answered by indicating the choice A, B, C or D by a stroke made in **ink** in the appropriate place in the answer sheet—see the sample question below.
4. For each question there is only **one** correct answer.
5. Rough working, if required, should be done only on this question paper—or on the rough working sheet provided—**not** on the answer sheet.
6. At the end of the examination the answer sheet for Section A **must** be placed inside the front cover of this answer book.

Sample Question

The apparatus used to determine the energy stored in a foodstuff is a

A respirometer
B calorimeter
C klinostat
D gas burette.

The correct answer is **B**—calorimeter. A **heavy** vertical line should be drawn joining the two dots in the appropriate box in the column headed **B** as shown in the example on the answer sheet.

If, after you have recorded your answer, you decide that you have made an error and wish to make a change, you should cancel the original answer and put a vertical stroke in the box you now consider to be correct. Thus, if you want to change an answer D to an answer B, your answer sheet would look like this:

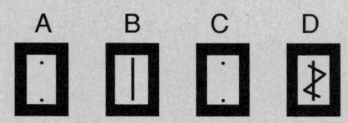

If you want to change back to an answer which has already been scored out, you should enter a tick (✓) to the **right** of the box of your choice, thus:

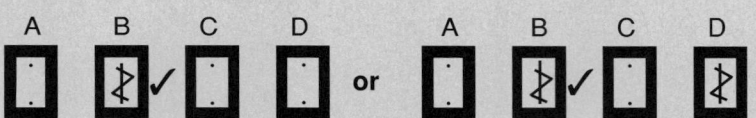

SECTION A

All questions in this section should be attempted.

Answers should be given on the separate answer sheet provided.

1. When an animal cell is immersed in a hypotonic solution it will
   A burst
   B become turgid
   C shrink
   D become flaccid.

2. In photosynthesis, the function of the pigment carotene is to
   A receive light energy from chlorophyll for photolysis of water
   B allow the plant to absorb a wider range of wavelengths of light
   C allow photosynthesis to take place in light of low intensity
   D increase the capacity of chlorophyll to absorb light.

3. On Earth, the energy input from sunlight is around 2.0×10^{12} kilojoules per hectare per annum. The energy captured by photosynthesising plants is around 2.0×10^{10} kilojoules per hectare per annum. (A hectare is a measurement of area.)

   What is the percentage efficiency of photosynthesis of these plants?
   A 1%
   B 2%
   C 17%
   D 200%

4. Three different strains of yeast each lacked a different respiratory enzyme involved in the complete breakdown of glucose.

   Strain X – cannot produce carbon dioxide from pyruvic acid.
   Strain Y – cannot form pyruvic acid.
   Strain Z – cannot reduce oxygen to form water.

   Which of the strains could produce ethanol?
   A Strains X and Y
   B Strains X and Z
   C Strain Y only
   D Strain Z only

5. Which of the following proteins has a fibrous structure?
   A Pepsin
   B Amylase
   C Insulin
   D Collagen

6. Insulin synthesised in a pancreatic cell is secreted from the cell. Its route from synthesis to secretion includes
   A Golgi apparatus → endoplasmic reticulum → ribosome
   B ribosome → Golgi apparatus → endoplasmic reticulum
   C endoplasmic reticulum → ribosome → Golgi apparatus
   D ribosome → endoplasmic reticulum → Golgi apparatus.

7. If a living tissue is transplanted from one person to another, there is a risk of rejection because the recipient reacts against the foreign
   A antibodies
   B antigens
   C DNA
   D RNA.

[Turn over

8. Which of the following cells are responsible for producing antibodies?

   A Monocytes
   B Lymphocytes
   C Phagocytes
   D Red blood cells

9. Viruses consist of a

   A lipid coat enclosing DNA or RNA
   B protein coat enclosing DNA only
   C protein coat enclosing DNA or RNA
   D lipid coat enclosing DNA only.

10. What is the significance of chiasma formation?

    A It results in the halving of the chromosome number.
    B It results in the pairing of homologous chromosomes.
    C It permits gene exchange between homologous chromosomes.
    D It results in the independent assortment of chromosomes.

11. The table below shows some genotypes and phenotypes associated with forms of sickle-cell anaemia.

Genotype	Phenotype
$Hb^A Hb^A$	normal
$Hb^A Hb^S$	sickle-cell trait
$Hb^S Hb^S$	acute sickle-cell anaemia

    A normal man marries a woman with the sickle-cell trait. What are the chances that any child born to them will have acute sickle-cell anaemia?

    A None
    B 1 in 1
    C 1 in 2
    D 1 in 4

12. The diagram shows the transmission of the gene for albinism.

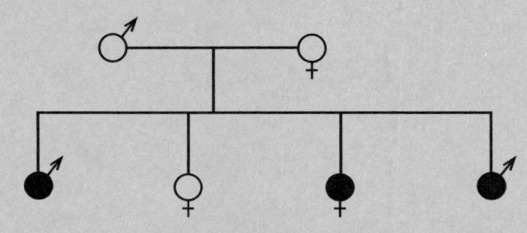

    Key
    normal male ○   affected male ●
    normal female ○   affected female ●

    This condition is inherited as a characteristic which is

    A dominant and not sex-linked
    B recessive and not sex-linked
    C dominant and sex-linked
    D recessive and sex-linked.

13. In *Drosophila*, the long-winged condition (L) is dominant to the vestigial-winged condition (l) and broad abdomen (B) is dominant to narrow abdomen (b).

    When parent flies, heterozygous for both wing shape and abdomen width, were crossed with flies having vestigial wings and narrow abdomens, the results were as shown in the table below.

	Number of male offspring	Number of female offspring
Long wings, broad abdomen	230	227
Long wings, narrow abdomen	4	3
Vestigial wings, broad abdomen	3	3
Vestigial wings, narrow abdomen	238	240

    These results indicate

    A crossing over
    B independent assortment
    C a mutation
    D sex-linkage.

14. Colour blindness is a recessive, sex-linked characteristic controlled by the allele b.

    Two parents with normal vision have a colour-blind boy.

    The genotypes of the parents are

    A X^BY and X^BX^b
    B X^bY and X^BX^B
    C X^bY and X^BX^b
    D X^BY and X^bX^b.

15. Which of the following mutations would cause a change in chromosome number?

    A Translocation
    B Non-disjunction
    C Inversion
    D Insertion

16. Genes **a** to **j** occur on part of a chromosome.

    | a | b | c | d | e | f | g | h | i | j |

    After cell division, this part of the chromosome had the following sequence of genes:

    | a | b | c | d | e | f | g | d | e | f | g | h | i | j |

    This change is called a

    A repetition
    B translocation
    C duplication
    D replication.

17. Cabbage and radish each have a diploid number of 18. These plants can be crossed to produce a hybrid.

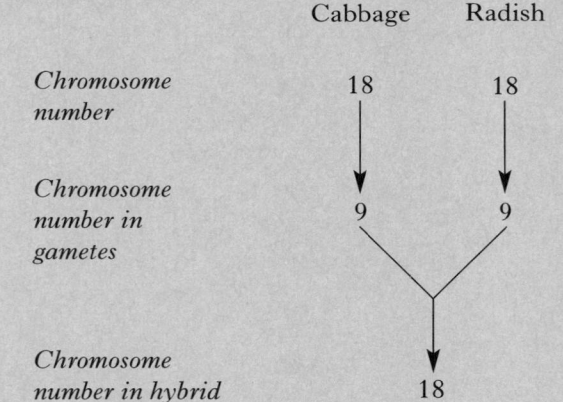

    Cabbage   Radish
    Chromosome number   18   18
    Chromosome number in gametes   9   9
    Chromosome number in hybrid   18

    Which of the following statements is true?

    A The hybrid contains 9 pairs of homologous chromosomes.
    B The chromosomes in the hybrid cannot pair during meiosis.
    C The hybrid can produce gametes with a haploid number of 9.
    D The hybrid can interbreed successfully with either parent.

18. In the formation of protoplasts, plant cells are treated with

    A amylase
    B lipase
    C restriction enzymes
    D cellulase.

19. Which of the following is an example of intraspecific competition?

    A Plants of the same species competing for the same growth requirements.
    B Plants of the same species competing for different growth requirements.
    C Plants of a different species competing for the same growth requirements.
    D Plants of a different species competing for different growth requirements.

[Turn over

20. In an animal, habituation has taken place when a

A harmful stimulus ceases to produce a response

B harmful stimulus always produces an identical response

C harmless stimulus always produces an identical response

D harmless stimulus ceases to produce a response.

21. The rates of carbon dioxide exchange by the leaves of two species of plants were measured at different light intensities.

The results are shown in the graph below.

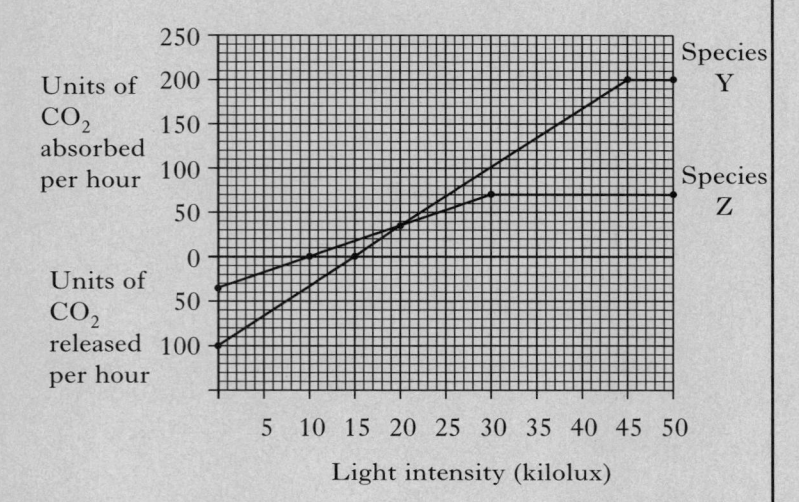

What are the light intensities at which species Z and Y reach their compensation points?

	Light Intensity (kilolux)	
	Z	Y
A	10	15
B	20	20
C	20	30
D	30	45

22. Which of the following statements explains the structural differences between cells in different tissues of an organism?

A Cells in some tissues have more genes than cells in other tissues.

B As different tissues develop, different genes are lost from their cells.

C Different cell types have the same genes but different genes are active.

D Some tissues have genes from one parent while some have genes from the other.

23. The thyroid gland is involved in the control of metabolic rate.

Which of the following shows the correct sequence for metabolic control.

A Pituitary → thyroxine → thyroid → TSH

B Pituitary → TSH → thyroid → thyroxine

C TSH → thyroxine → pituitary → thyroid

D Thyroid → TSH → thyroxine → pituitary

24. Which of the following is the correct sequence of events that occurs in control of the concentration of blood sugar?

	Concentration of blood sugar	Glucagon secretion	Insulin secretion	Glycogen stored in liver
A	increases	decreases	increases	increases
B	increases	decreases	increases	decreases
C	decreases	increases	decreases	increases
D	decreases	decreases	increases	decreases

25. Which of the following is **not** the result of a magnesium deficiency in flowering plants?

A Curling of the leaves

B Yellowing of the leaves

C Reduction in shoot growth

D Reduction in root growth

26. A 30 g serving of breakfast cereal with 125 cm³ of semi-skimmed milk contains 1·5 mg of iron. Only 25% of this iron is absorbed into the bloodstream.

If a woman in late pregnancy requires a daily intake of 6 mg of iron, how much cereal and milk would have to be eaten to meet this requirement?

	Cereal (g)	Milk (cm³)
A	60	250
B	120	500
C	240	1000
D	480	2000

27. In humans, vitamin D plays an essential role in the absorption of

A glucose

B calcium

C iron

D lipids.

28. Which one of the following factors affecting a population of rabbits is density independent?

A Viral disease

B The population of foxes

C The biomass of the grass

D Rainfall

29. The diagram shows the average lifespan of people in Britain between 1900 and 1990.

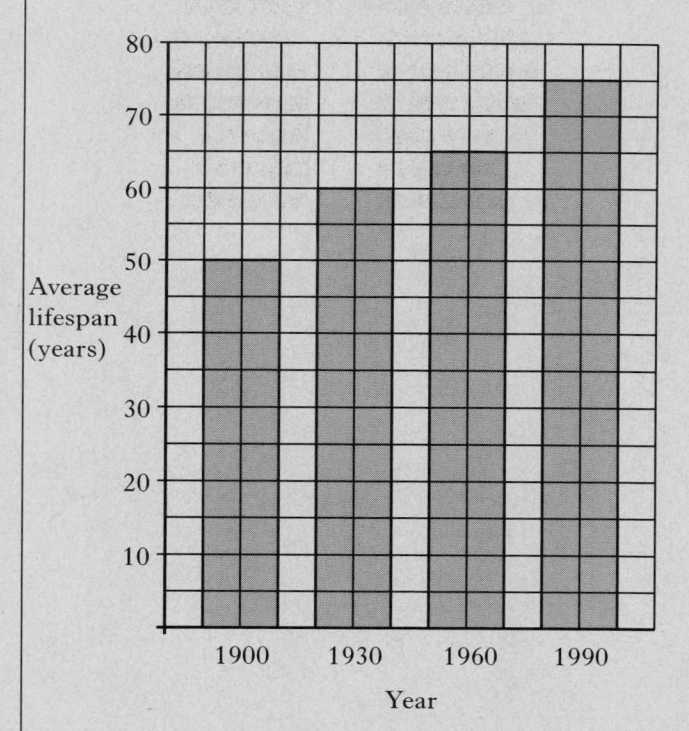

What is the percentage increase in lifespan during this period?

A 25%

B 45%

C 50%

D 75%

30. The graphs below contain information about the population of Britain.

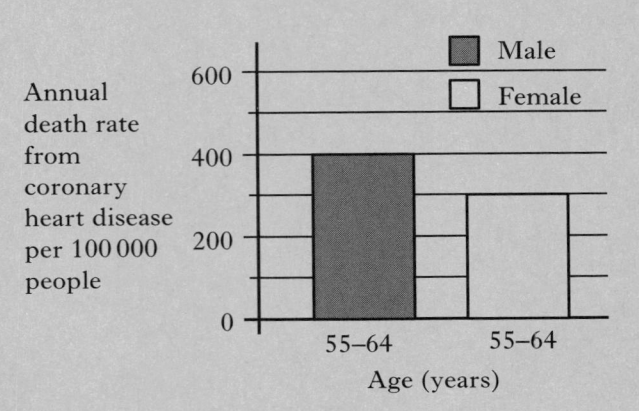

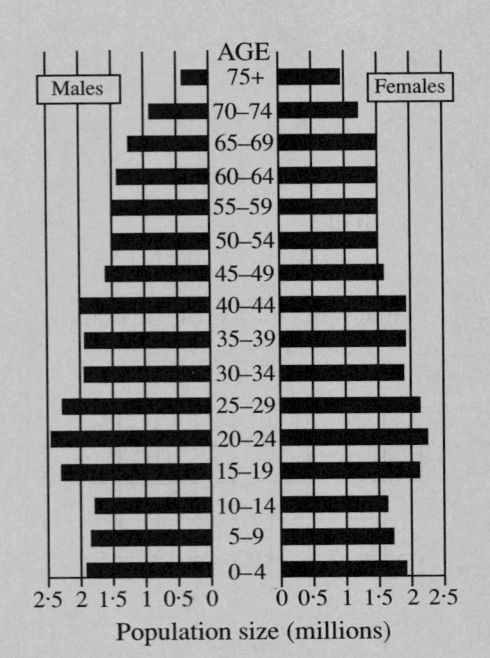

How many British women between 55 and 64 years of age die from coronary heart disease annually?

A   300

B   4500

C   9000

D   21 000

[Turn over for Section B on *Page ten*

SECTION B

All questions in this section should be attempted.

1. The diagram below represents stages in aerobic respiration in mammalian liver cells.

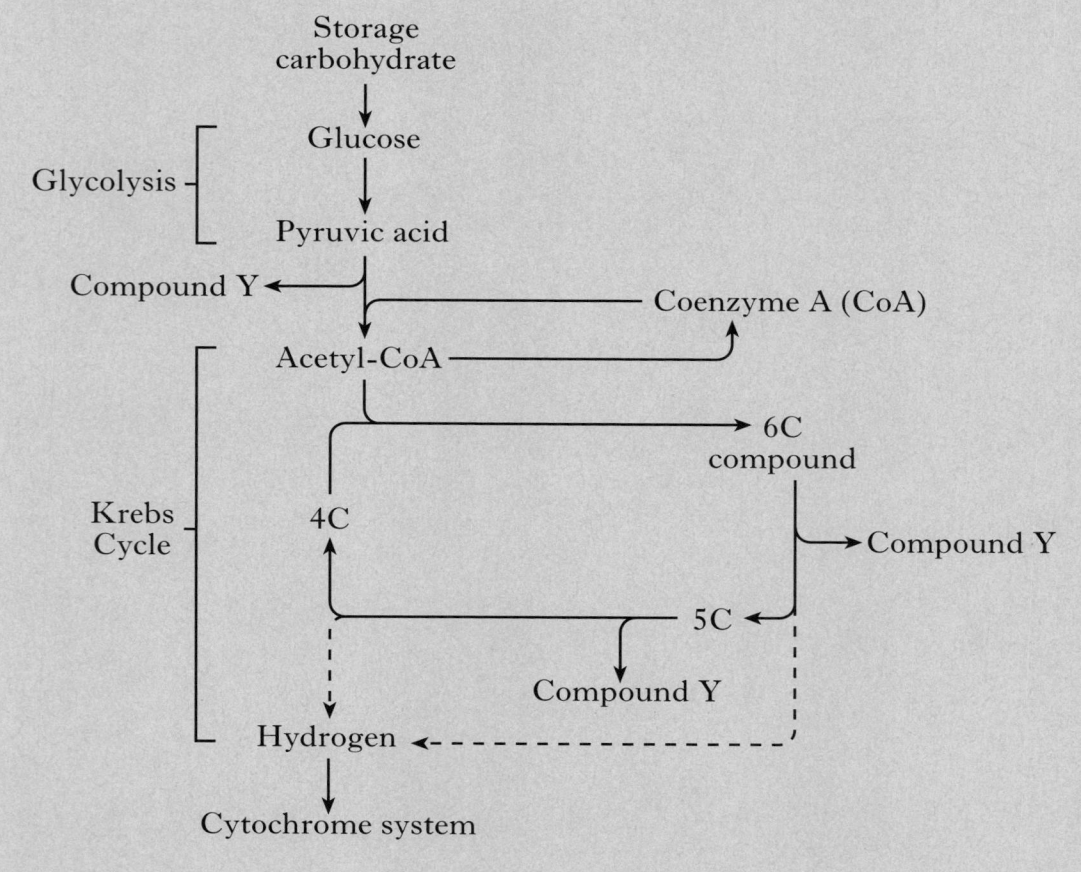

    (a) Name the storage carbohydrate in liver cells.

    _____

    (b) Other than carbohydrate, name an alternative respiratory substrate.

    _____

    (c) State the exact location within a liver cell of:

    1 Glycolysis _____

    2 Krebs cycle _____

    (d) State the net gain of ATP molecules from the breakdown of a glucose molecule to pyruvic acid.

    _____

1. (continued)

(e) Name the 6 carbon compound and compound Y shown in the Krebs cycle.

6C compound _____

Compound Y _____

(f) Name the chemical that transports hydrogen from the Krebs cycle to the cytochrome system.

_____

[Turn over

2. (a) The graph below shows the effects of varying light intensity, carbon dioxide concentration and temperature on the rate of photosynthesis in a plant.

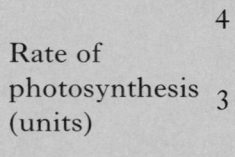

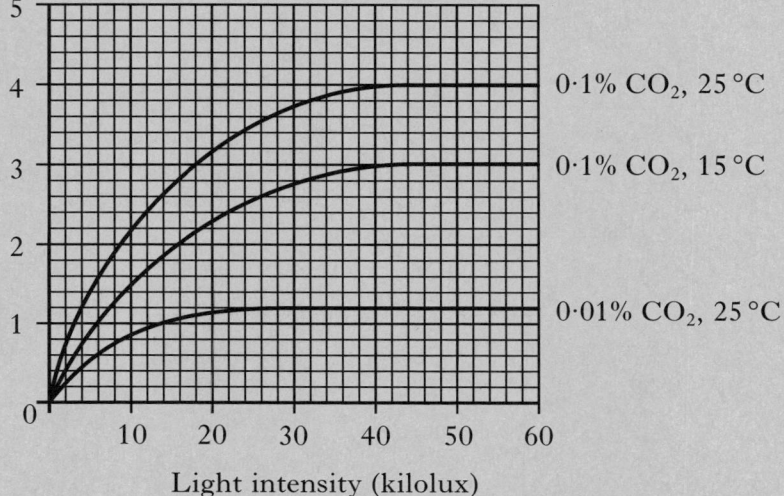

[Graph: Rate of photosynthesis (units) vs Light intensity (kilolux), showing three curves:
- 0·1% CO_2, 25 °C (levels off at ~4)
- 0·1% CO_2, 15 °C (levels off at ~3)
- 0·01% CO_2, 25 °C (levels off at ~1·2)]

(i) At a light intensity of 60 kilolux, identify which factor, as shown in the graph, has the greater effect in increasing the rate of photosynthesis. Justify your answer.

Factor _____

Justification _____

_____

_____ **1**

(ii) The experiment was repeated at a carbon dioxide concentration of 0·01% and a temperature of 15 °C. **Onto the graph above**, draw a curve to show the predicted results of this experiment. **1**

(iii) The rate of photosynthesis can be calculated by measuring a change in dry mass with time.
State **one** other method that can be used to calculate the rate of photosynthesis.

_____

_____ **1**

(b) Other than being absorbed for use in photosynthesis, give **two** possible fates of the light energy that shines onto the leaves of plants.

1 _____

2 _____ **1**

(c) Within which region of a chloroplast does the absorption of light take place?

_____ **1**

2. (continued)

(d) Name the **two** chemical compounds produced in the light dependent stage that are essential for the conversion of GP to glucose.

Compound 1 _____

Compound 2 _____ 1

(e) Complete the table below by inserting the number of carbon atoms present in each of the chemical compounds.

Compound	Number of carbon atoms
GP	
RuBP	
Glucose	

1

(f) What would be the effect on the RuBP concentration if conditions were changed from light with carbon dioxide present to light with carbon dioxide absent.
Explain your answer.

Effect _____

Explanation _____

_____

_____ 2

(g) The list below shows terms which refer to the role of light in the growth and development of plants and animals.

List of terms
Phototropism
Compensation point
Etiolation
Photoperiodism

In the table below insert the term that is described by each statement.

Statement	Term
The rate of respiration equals the rate of photosynthesis at a certain light intensity.	
If germinated in darkness, a seedling has long internodes and small yellow leaves.	
Plants respond to directional light by a growth curvature.	
A change in the number of hours of light in the day can affect growth and development in many plants and animals.	

2

3. (*a*) Bar graph 1 shows the concentrations of sodium and potassium in the cell sap of a water plant and in the surrounding pond water.
The data were collected at 20 °C under aerobic conditions.

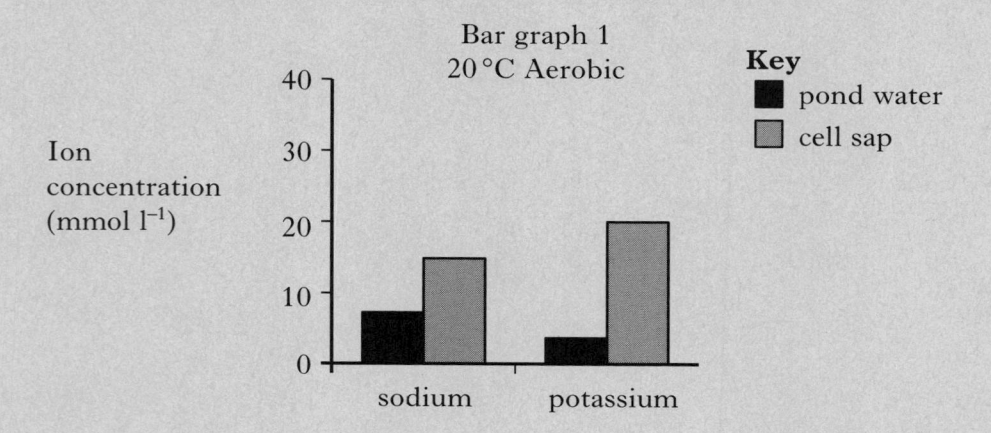

Bar graph 1
20 °C Aerobic

Key
■ pond water
□ cell sap

Ion concentration (mmol l^{-1})

(i) What evidence from the bar graph suggests that:

1 ion uptake is by active transport? _____

_____ 1

2 ion uptake is selective? _____

_____ 1

The experiment was repeated at different temperatures and oxygen availability. The results obtained are shown below.

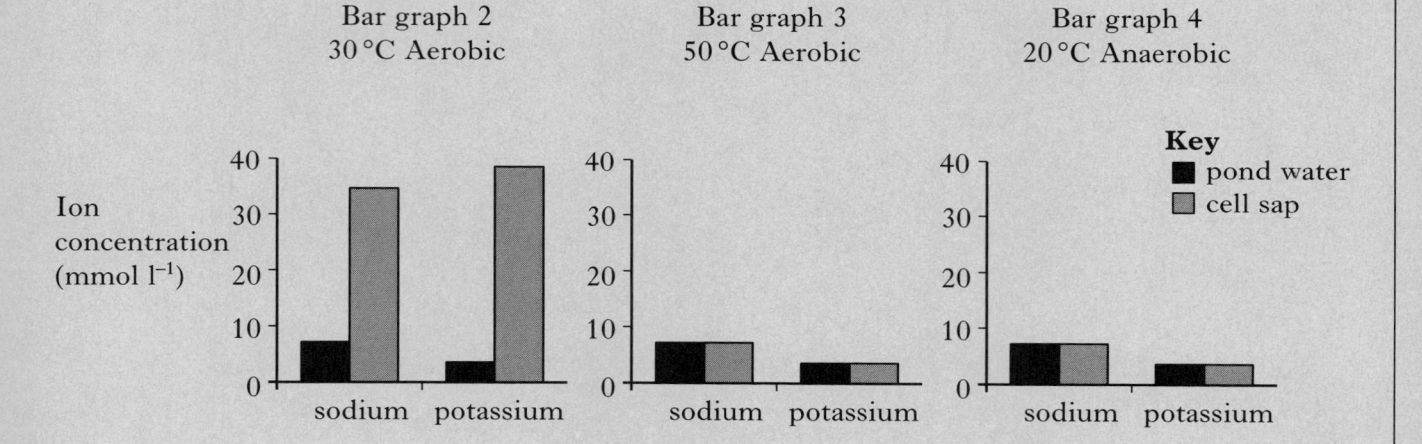

Bar graph 2
30 °C Aerobic

Bar graph 3
50 °C Aerobic

Bar graph 4
20 °C Anaerobic

Key
■ pond water
□ cell sap

Ion concentration (mmol l^{-1})

3. *(a)* **(continued)**

   (ii) Complete the table below to identify **two** bar graphs which could be compared to support each statement.

Statement	Comparison	
	Bar graph number	Bar graph number
Enzyme activity increases with increasing temperature		
Membrane proteins may be denatured		

   (iii) Account for the differences in ion uptake shown in bar graphs 1 and 4.

   _____

   _____

   _____

(b) State the importance of potassium in the normal functioning of plant cells.

   _____

   _____

[Turn over

4. (*a*) A gamete mother cell undergoes meiosis to form gametes.
The bar graph below shows the DNA content per cell at different stages in meiosis.

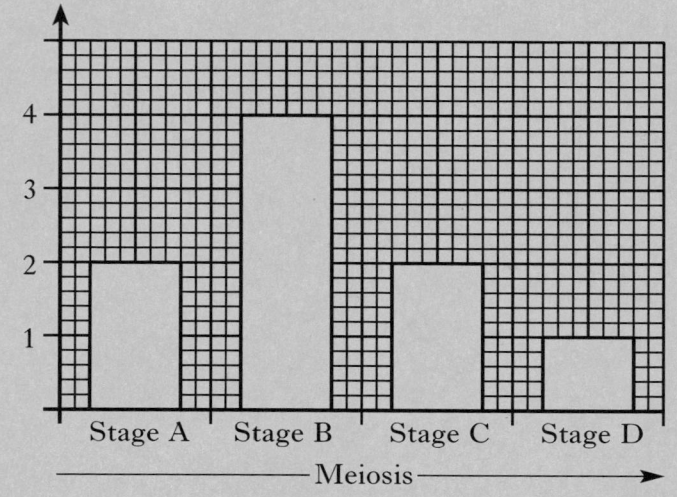

Describe what happens during meiosis to account for the change in the DNA content per cell between the following stages.

1 Stages A and B _____

_____ 1

2 Stages B and C _____

_____ 1

3 Stages C and D _____

_____ 1

(*b*) The table below shows the percentage recombination frequencies for four genes present on the same chromosome.

Gene pairs	% recombination frequency
P and Q	16
P and R	8
R and S	12
Q and S	4

(i) What term is used to describe genes present on the same chromosome?

_____ 1

(ii) Use the information to identify the order in which these genes lie on the chromosome.

Space for calculation

Order _____ 1

5. (*a*) Cyanogenic clover plants produce cyanide when their tissues are damaged. Cyanide is toxic and its production defends plants against herbivores.
The diagram below shows the metabolic pathway which produces cyanide.

Substrate A ---------→ Substrate B ---------→ cyanide
            ↑   ↑
     Enzyme 1   Enzyme 2

The genes which code for Enzymes 1 and 2 have alleles with properties shown in the table below.

Gene coding for Enzyme 1		Gene coding for Enzyme 2	
Allele	Synthesises Enzyme 1	Allele T	Synthesises Enzyme 2
Allele r	Cannot synthesise Enzyme 1	Allele t	Cannot synthesise Enzyme 2

(i) Complete the cross below by:

1. inserting the genotype of the gametes of the individual with the genotype RrTt;

2. showing the possible genotypes of the offspring.

Parental phenotypes   Cyanogenic   X   Non-cyanogenic
Parental genotypes   RrTt   X   rrtt

Gamete(s) →				
(rt)				

(ii) Express the expected number of cyanogenic to non-cyanogenic plants as the simplest whole number ratio.

Ratio   cyanogenic _____ : non-cyanogenic _____

(*b*) Give **two** examples of adaptions which allow plants to tolerate grazing.

Example 1 _____

Example 2 _____

[Turn over

6. (*a*) The following statements refer to the Hawaiian islands and species which inhabit them.

Statements

1. The Hawaiian islands are of volcanic origin.
2. The islands are far from any continental mainland.
3. 91% of the plant species and 81% of the bird species are found only on these islands.
4. Hawaiian honeycreepers are species of birds which are descended from a seed-eating ancestral species.
5. Honeycreeper species show a wide range of beak shapes for eating the seeds, fruits, nectar and insects available.
6. Estimates of the present number of honeycreeper species range from 29 to 33 with many extinctions having occurred after the arrival of man on the islands.

(i) Name the isolation mechanism illustrated in Statement 2.

_____ 1

(ii) State the importance of isolating mechanisms in the evolution of new species.

_____
_____
_____ 1

(iii) Identify the **two** statements which suggest that the evolution of the honeycreeper species is an example of adaptive radiation.

Statement numbers _____ and _____ 1

(iv) Name **two** methods used to conserve species and prevent their extinction. (Statement 6)

_____
_____
_____ 2

6. (continued)

(b) Populations may be monitored to provide data for a wide variety of purposes. The table below shows the sulphur dioxide concentrations within various areas and the number of lichen species present.

Sulphur dioxide concentration in area (ppm)	Number of lichen species present
32	0
17	4
8	11
0	17

From the table explain how lichen can be used as indicator species.

_____

_____

_____   1

(c) Explain the need to monitor populations of fish such as cod.

_____

_____

_____   1

[Turn over

7. The bacterium *Bacillus thuringiensis* produces a substance called T-toxin that is harmful to leaf-eating insects.

The information below shows some of the procedures used by genetic engineers to insert the gene for the production of T-toxin into crop plants.

Procedure 1   Chromosome extracted from bacterial cells

Procedure 2   Position of T-toxin gene located

Procedure 3   T-toxin gene cut out from bacterial chromosome

Procedure 4   T-toxin gene transferred into nucleus of host plant cell

Procedure 5   Plant cells containing T-toxin gene grown into plantlets

(a) Name a technique that could be used in Procedure 2 to locate the position of the T-toxin gene.

_____

(b) Name the enzyme used in procedure 3.

_____

(c) Explain why such genetically engineered crop plants would grow better than unmodified crop plants.

_____

_____

_____

(d) These crops were commercially successful for several years. However, they have since become susceptible to attack by some members of a particular insect species.

Suggest a reason that would account for this observation.

_____

_____

8. The flowchart represents the control system involved in returning body temperature to normal after an increase.

Increase in body temperature
↓
Increase detected by temperature-monitoring centre
↓
Corrective mechanisms switched on
↓
Return to normal body temperature
↓
Decrease detected by temperature-monitoring centre
↓
Corrective mechanisms switched off

(a) State the exact location of the temperature-monitoring centre.

_____ 1

(b) In the following sentence **underline** one of the alternatives in each pair to describe a corrective mechanism that is switched on when body temperature increases.

In this corrective mechanism {vasoconstriction / vasodilation} results in {increased / decreased} blood flow to the skin and therefore, {increased / decreased} heat loss from the skin by radiation. 1

(c) Describe another corrective mechanism that would reduce body temperature.

_____
_____ 1

(d) How is the message carried from the temperature-monitoring centre to effectors?

_____ 1

(e) What is the importance of body temperature in humans to metabolic processes?

_____
_____ 1

9. An investigation was carried out into the effect of different concentrations of indole-acetic acid (IAA) on growth of shoot tips.

The method used in the investigation is outlined below.

1. 10 mm lengths of shoot tissue were cut from behind the shoot tip meristem.
2. Five lengths of shoot tissue were used in each experiment.
3. Shoot tissues were immersed in solutions containing different concentrations of IAA.
4. The diagram below shows the experimental set up at one of the concentrations of IAA.

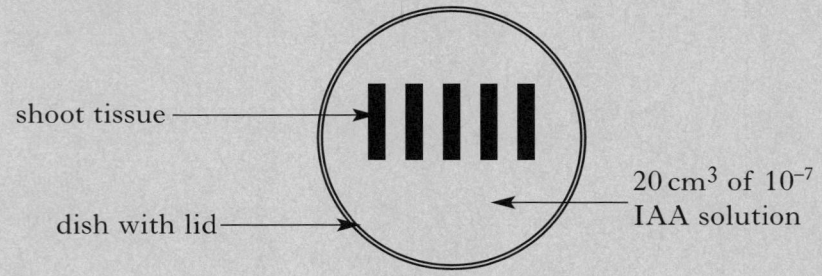

shoot tissue

dish with lid

20 cm^3 of 10^{-7} IAA solution

5. A control experiment was set up with five 10 mm lengths of intact shoot tip tissue immersed in distilled water.
6. The experiments were left in the dark for 48 hours.
7. The length of each shoot tip tissue was measured.
8. For each IAA concentration, the average length of shoot tip tissue was compared with the control experiment.

Key

+ Growth greater than control

– Growth less than control

The results are shown in the table below.

Concentration of IAA solution (molar)	Difference between the average length of shoot tissue and the control (mm)
10^{-7}	+4
10^{-6}	+8
10^{-5}	+5
10^{-4}	+3
10^{-3}	0
10^{-2}	–2
10^{-1}	–4

[Question 9 continues on *Page twenty-three* and fold-out *Page twenty-four*

9. (continued)

(a) On the grid below, using a suitable scale, plot a line graph of difference between the average length of shoot tissue and the control against concentration of IAA solution.
(Additional graph paper, if required, can be found on *Page thirty-two*.)

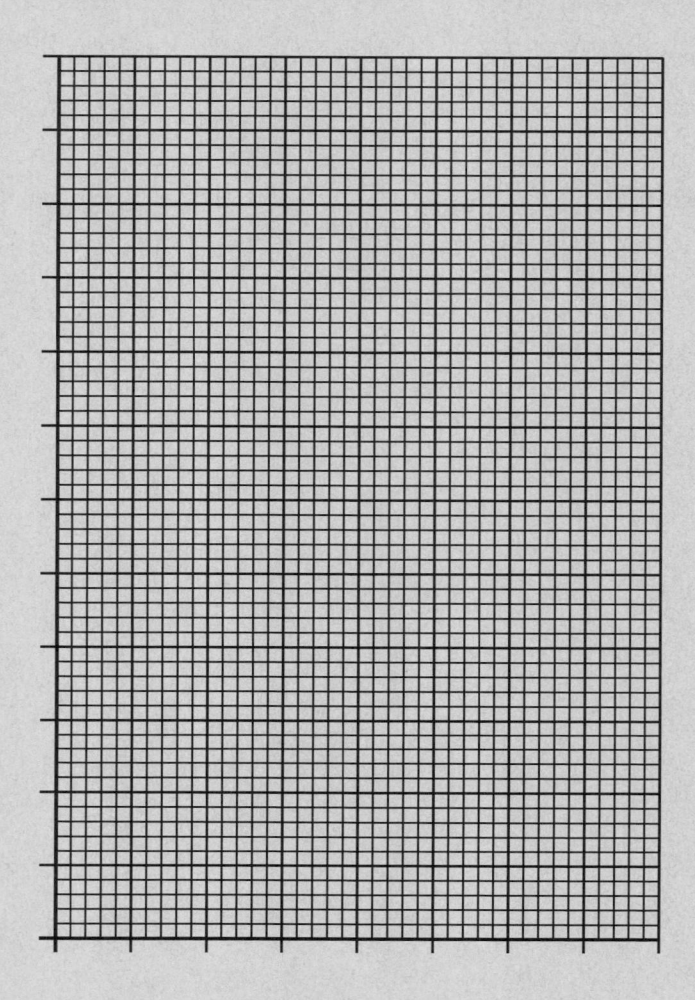

2

(b) Describe the pattern of growth of shoot tissue over the range of IAA concentrations used in the investigation.

_____

_____

_____

2

(c) Why is it considered good experimental procedure to leave the shoot tissues in the solutions for 48 hours?

_____

_____

1

[Question 9 continues on *Page twenty-four*

9. (continued)

(d) All the IAA solutions were measured using the same syringe. What precaution should be taken to minimise experimental error?

_____

_____ **1**

(e) In this investigation what would appear to be the naturally occurring concentration of IAA within the shoot tip?

_____

_____ **1**

[*Question 10 begins on fold-out Page twenty-five*

10. The red spider mite is a pest of crop plants. Stages in its life-cycle are shown in the diagram below.

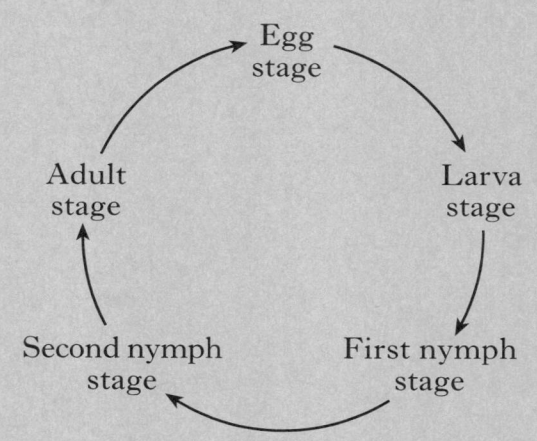

Egg stage → Larva stage → First nymph stage → Second nymph stage → Adult stage → Egg stage

An investigation was carried out into the effects of temperature on the time each of the early stages lasts. The results are shown in the bar graph below.

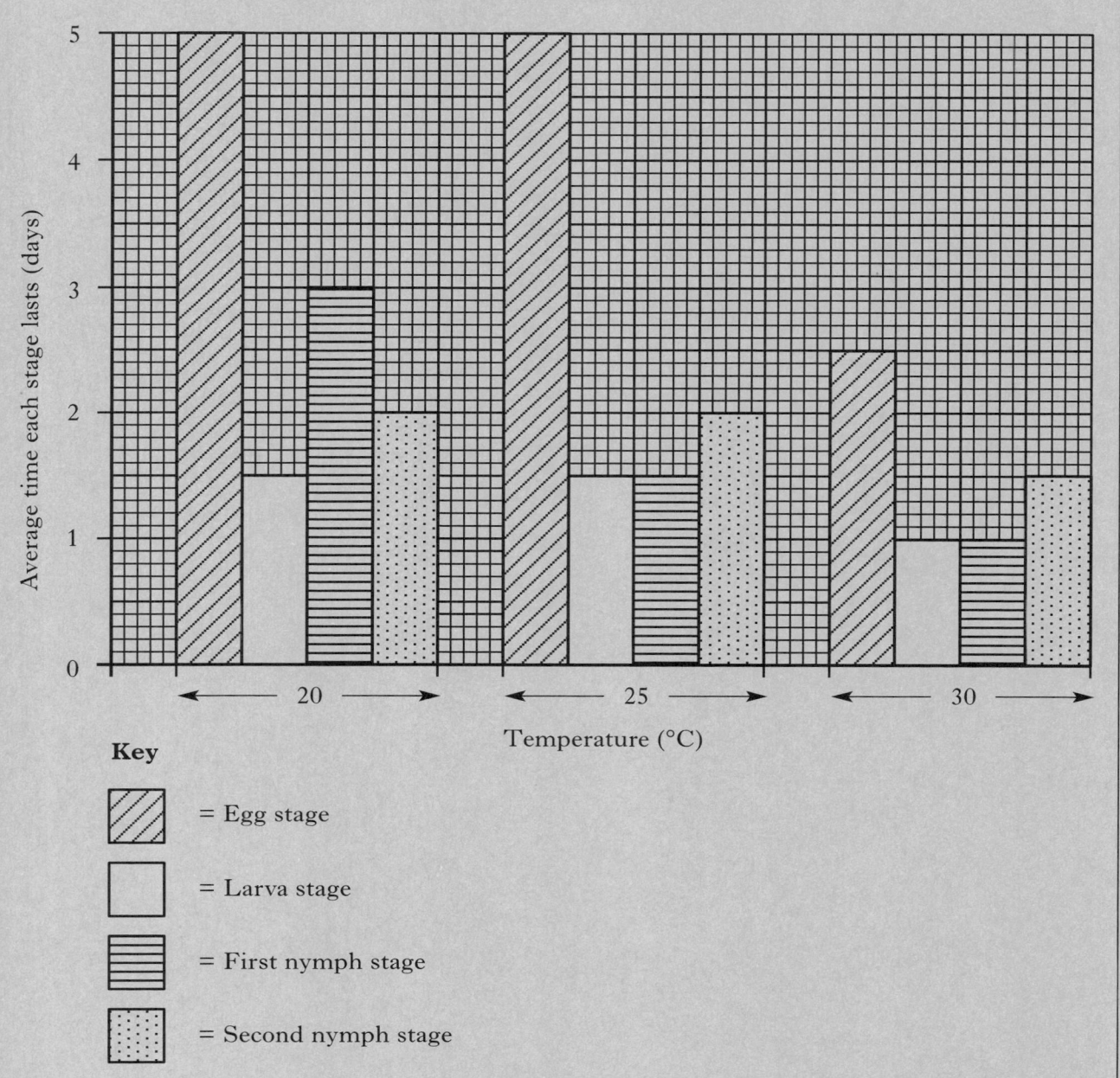

Key

- ▨ = Egg stage
- ▢ = Larva stage
- ▤ = First nymph stage
- ▦ = Second nymph stage

10. (continued)

(a) From the bar graph, calculate the difference in average time for development through the egg stage to the start of the adult stage at 20 °C and 30 °C.

Space for calculation

Difference _____ days

Table 1 below shows the effect of temperature on features of egg laying in adult red spider mites.

Table 1

Features	Temperature (°C)		
	20 °C	25 °C	30 °C
Average time spent as an adult before first egg laid (days)	2·20	1·60	1·00
Average length of egg laying period (days)	18·40	14·80	10·36
Average number of eggs laid per female during egg laying period	92·00	88·80	62·16

(b) From Table 1, describe the relationship between temperature and each feature of egg-laying in adult female red spider mites.

_____

_____

_____

_____

(c) From Table 1, calculate the average number of eggs laid per female per day during the egg laying period at 20 °C.

Space for calculation

Average number of eggs laid per female per day _____

10. (continued)

(d) From Table 1, calculate the percentage decrease in the average number of eggs laid per female during the egg laying period when the temperature is increased from 25 °C to 30 °C.

Space for calculation

% decrease _____   1

(e) From the information in the bar graph and Table 1, complete the table below by writing **True** or **False** in each of the spaces provided.

Statement	True/False
The time for the length of the first nymph stage is shortest at 30 °C.	
The egg stage lasts twice as long at 30 °C as at 25 °C.	
Only the first nymph stage is affected by a change from 20 °C to 25 °C.	
At 20 °C some adults may take more than 2·2 days to start laying eggs.	

2

(f) From the bar graph and Table 1, calculate the average time that it takes for development from the egg stage to the laying of the first egg at 25 °C.

Space for calculation

Average time _____ days   1

[Turn over

11. (a) The graph below shows changes in stomatal width over a 24-hour period of a plant species that is adapted to live in a hot climate.

Average stomatal width (units) vs Time (hours)

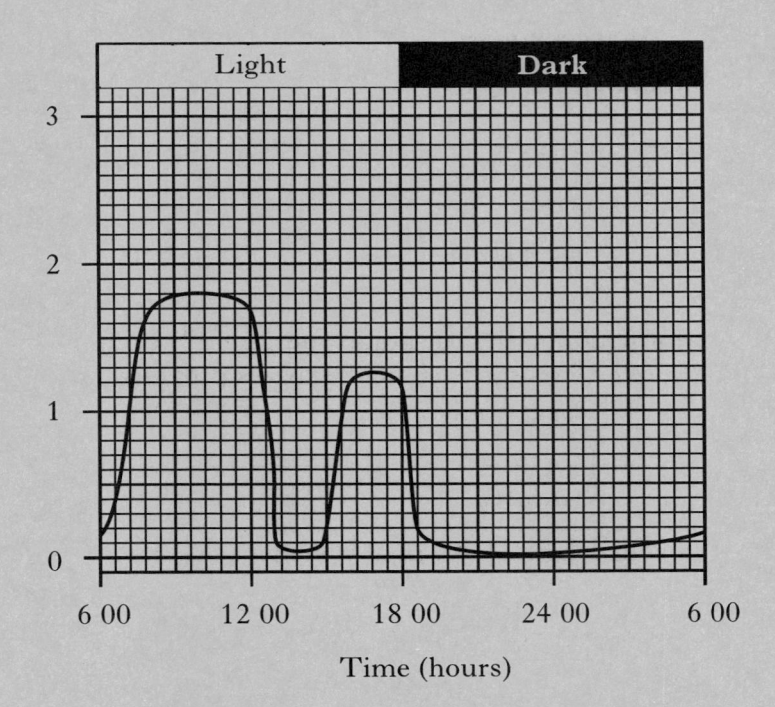

(i) State the change in turgor that takes place in the guard cells to cause stomatal closure.

_____

(ii) 1 Explain how the pattern of change in stomatal width between 11 00 and 16 00 may benefit a plant that lives in a hot climate.

_____

_____

_____

2 Suggest a possible disadvantage to the plant of this pattern of change in stomatal width.

_____

_____

11. (continued)

(b) Plants that live in desert conditions have adaptations which reduce water loss. The diagram below shows part of a leaf section of a desert plant.

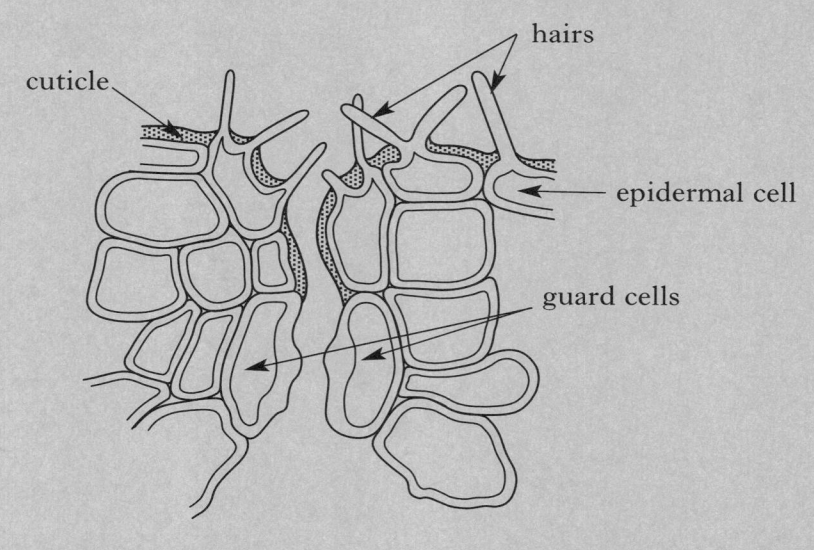

Complete the table below which shows leaf adaptations and explanations of how these reduce water loss.

Description of adaptation	Explanation for reduction in water loss
Presence of hairs on the leaf surface	
	Longer distance for water vapour to diffuse out of the leaf.

Marks: 2

(c) Salmon and eels have adaptations associated with migration between freshwater and seawater.

(i) State the change that takes place in the glomerular filtration rate of these fish when they return to the sea.

_____ *1*

(ii) Describe the role of the chloride secretory cells when these fish are in seawater.

_____ *1*

(d) Describe **one** behavioural and **one** physiological adaptation shown by the desert rat to reduce water loss.

Behavioural _____

_____ *1*

Physiological _____

_____ *1*

12. (a) The diagram below represents a section through a woody stem.

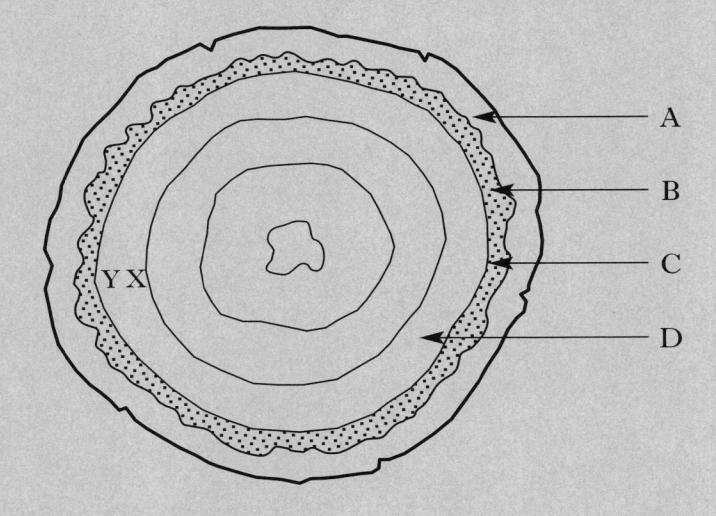

(i) Name the lateral meristem in a woody stem.

_____

(ii) Which letter identifies this tissue?

Letter _____

(b) State whether the average diameter of the vessels in area X would be larger or smaller than those in area Y. Give a reason for your choice.

Average diameter of vessels in area X compared to area Y _____

Reason _____

_____

SECTION C

Both questions in this section should be attempted.

Note that each question contains a choice.

Questions 1 and 2 should be attempted on the blank pages which follow.

Supplementary sheets, if required, may be obtained from the invigilator.

Labelled diagrams may be used where appropriate.

1. Answer **either** A **or** B.

    A. Write notes on each of the following:

    (i) the structure of the plasma membrane; **3**

    (ii) the structure and function of the cell wall; **3**

    (iii) phagocytosis. **4**

    (10)

    OR

    B. Write notes on each of the following:

    (i) mRNA synthesis; **5**

    (ii) the role of mRNA in protein synthesis. **5**

    (10)

In question 2, ONE mark is available for coherence and ONE mark is available for relevance.

2. Answer **either** A **or** B.

    A. Give an account of the Jacob-Monod hypothesis of lactose metabolism in Escherichia coli and the part played by genes in the condition of phenylketonuria. **(10)**

    OR

    B. Give an account of the effects of IAA on plant growth and the role of gibberellic acid in α-amylase induction in barley grains. **(10)**

[END OF QUESTION PAPER]

[Turn over

Official SQA Past Papers: Higher Biology 2002

SPACE FOR ANSWERS

ADDITIONAL GRAPH PAPER FOR QUESTION 9(a)

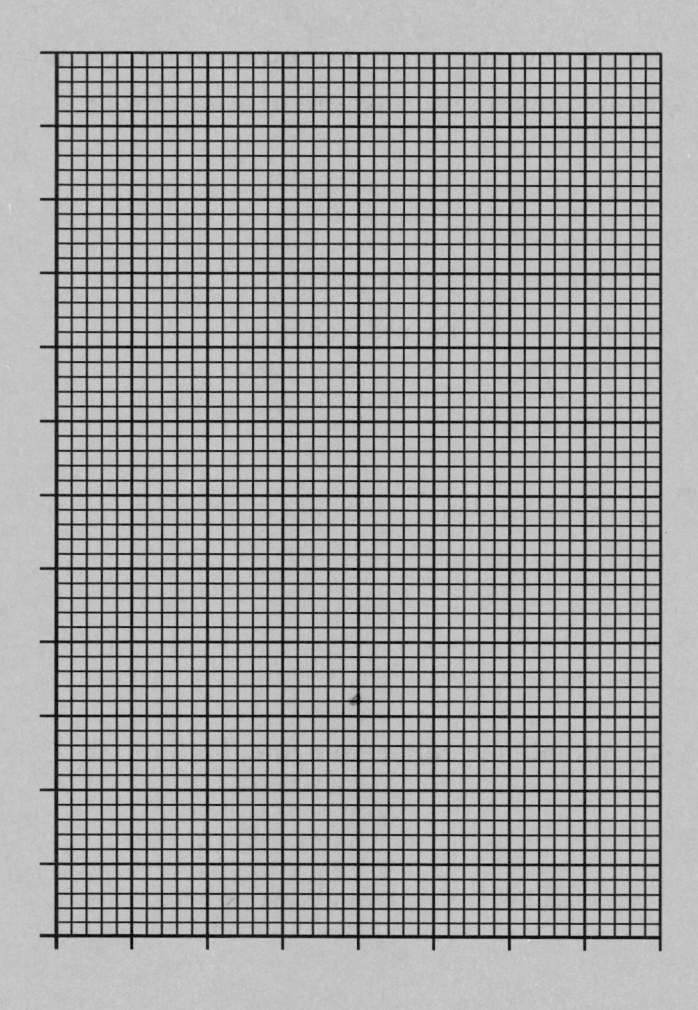

FOR OFFICIAL USE

Total for Sections B and C

W007/301

NATIONAL QUALIFICATIONS 2002

WEDNESDAY, 16 JANUARY
9.00 AM – 11.30 AM

BIOLOGY HIGHER

Fill in these boxes and read what is printed below.

Full name of centre

Town

Forename(s)

Surname

Date of birth
Day Month Year

Scottish candidate number

Number of seat

SECTION A—Questions 1–30 (30 marks)
Instructions for completion of Section A are given on page two.

SECTIONS B AND C (100 marks)

1. (a) All questions should be attempted.
   (b) It should be noted that in **Section C** questions 1 and 2 each contain a choice.

2. The questions may be answered in any order but all answers are to be written in the spaces provided in this answer book, and must be written clearly and legibly in ink.

3. Additional space for answers and rough work will be found at the end of the book. If further space is required, supplementary sheets may be obtained from the invigilator and should be inserted inside the **front** cover of this book.

4. The numbers of questions must be clearly inserted with any answers written in the additional space.

5. Rough work, if any should be necessary, should be written in this book and then scored through when the fair copy has been written.

6. Before leaving the examination room you must give this book to the invigilator. If you do not, you may lose all the marks for this paper.

SECTION A

Read carefully

1. Check that the answer sheet provided is for Biology Higher (Section A).
2. Fill in the details required on the answer sheet.
3. In this section a question is answered by indicating the choice A, B, C or D by a stroke made in **ink** in the appropriate place in the answer sheet—see the sample question below.
4. For each question there is only **one** correct answer.
5. Rough working, if required, should be done only on this question paper—or on the rough working sheet provided—**not** on the answer sheet.
6. At the end of the examination the answer sheet for Section A **must** be placed inside the front cover of this answer book.

Sample Question

The apparatus used to determine the energy stored in a foodstuff is a

A   respirometer
B   calorimeter
C   klinostat
D   gas burette.

The correct answer is **B**—calorimeter. A **heavy** vertical line should be drawn joining the two dots in the appropriate box in the column headed **B** as shown in the example on the answer sheet.

If, after you have recorded your answer, you decide that you have made an error and wish to make a change, you should cancel the original answer and put a vertical stroke in the box you now consider to be correct. Thus, if you want to change an answer D to an answer B, your answer sheet would look like this:

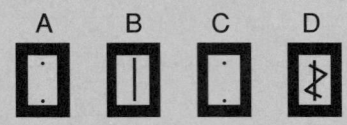

If you want to change back to an answer which has already been scored out, you should enter a tick (✓) to the **right** of the box of your choice, thus:

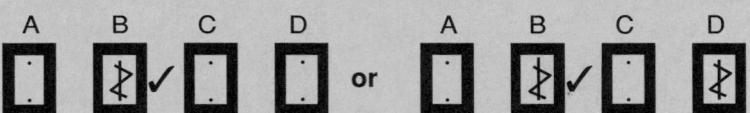

SECTION A

All questions in this section should be attempted.

Answers should be given on the separate answer sheet provided.

1. Which of the following correctly describes a chloroplast?

   A Bound by a single membrane with chlorophyll in the grana

   B Bound by a single membrane with chlorophyll in the stroma

   C Bound by a double membrane with chlorophyll in the grana

   D Bound by a double membrane with chlorophyll in the stroma

2. The diagram below shows the appearance of a plant cell which had been placed in an isotonic solution.

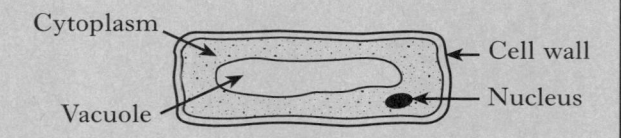

   Which of the following diagrams best illustrates the cell after being immersed in a hypertonic solution?

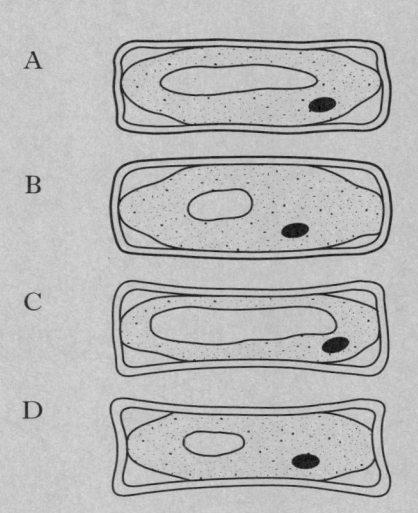

   A

   B

   C

   D

3. Which of the following statements about a young cell wall is **true**?

   A It is living.

   B It is composed mainly of cellulose.

   C It is composed mainly of protein.

   D It is selectively permeable.

4. Human red blood cells contain potassium ions at a concentration about 30 times greater than the concentration of potassium ions in the blood plasma. If red blood cells are cooled, potassium ions are lost to the surrounding plasma.

   If the cells are warmed again to body temperature, they regain their original concentration of potassium ions.

   These movements of potassium ions are explained by

	Outward movement	Inward movement
A	diffusion	active transport
B	diffusion	osmosis
C	active transport	diffusion
D	osmosis	active transport

5. In which of the following metabolic pathways is carbon dioxide taken up by ribulose bisphosphate (RuBP)?

   A Krebs cycle

   B Calvin cycle

   C Glycolysis

   D Photolysis

6. Assume that, to produce 1 unit of sugar by photosynthesis, each of the plants referred to in the following table had to receive

   - 2 units of carbon dioxide
   - 2 units of water
   - 4 units of light energy.

   In which plant was photosynthesis limited by the amount of CO_2 available?

Plant	Units of CO_2 available to plant	Units of H_2O available to plant	Units of light available to plant
A	4	4	7
B	6	8	16
C	4	8	4
D	6	8	11

7. The graphs below show the effect of two injections of an antigen on the formation of an antibody.

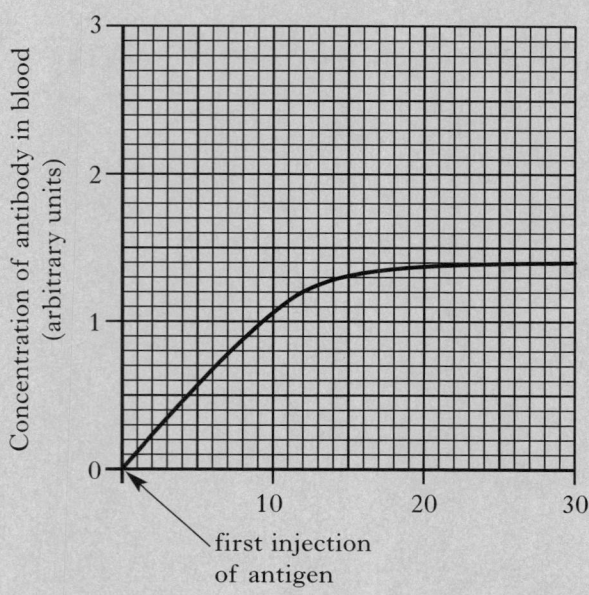

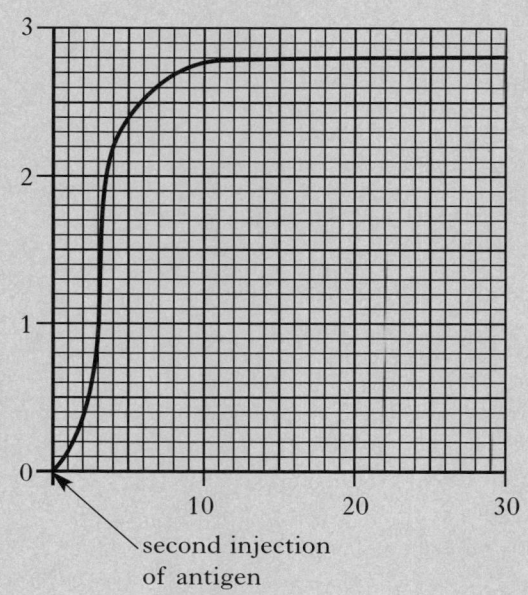

The concentration of antibodies is measured 25 days after each injection. The effect of the second injection is to increase the concentration by

A 1%

B 25%

C 50%

D 100%.

---

8. The following information refers to protein synthesis.

tRNA anticodon	amino acid carried by tRNA
GUG	Histidine (his)
CGU	Alanine (ala)
GCA	Arginine (arg)
AUG	Tyrosine (tyr)
UAC	Methionine (met)
UGU	Threonine (thr)

What order of amino acids would be synthesised from the base sequence of DNA shown below?

Base sequence of DNA: G C A A T G G T G

A arg – tyr – his

B ala – met – his

C ala – tyr – his

D arg – tyr – thr

9. Which of the following adaptations allow a plant to tolerate grazing by herbivores?

A Thick waxy cuticle

B Low meristems

C Leaves reduced to spines

D Thorny stems

10. Which of the following is **not** a plant response to invasion by other organisms?

A The formation of resin

B The production of nicotine

C The production of antibodies

D The production of tannins

11. The following diagram shows a homologous pair of chromosomes and the loci of 4 genes.

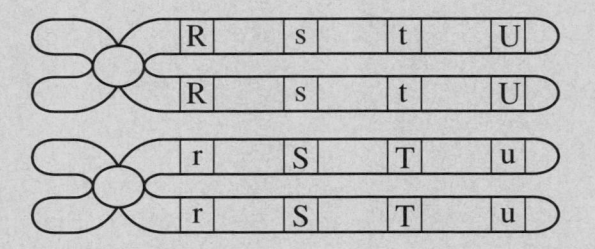

R	s	t	U
R	s	t	U
r	S	T	u
r	S	T	u

Chiasma formation would occur least often between genes

A r and t

B r and s

C r and U

D s and u.

12. The relative positions of the genes M, N, O and P on a chromosome were determined by the analysis of percentage recombination. The results are shown in the table.

Genes	Percentage recombination
M and O	10
N and O	27
N and P	12
M and P	29

The correct order of genes on the chromosome is

A O M P N

B M N O P

C M O N P

D O M N P.

13. Colour blindness is a sex-linked condition. John, who is colour-blind, has the family tree shown below.

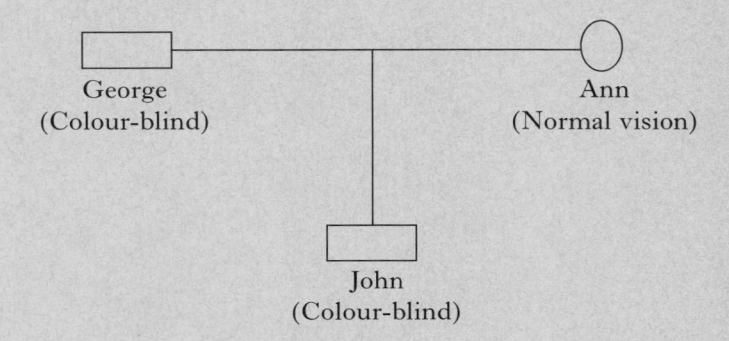

George (Colour-blind) — Ann (Normal vision)

John (Colour-blind)

If X^b is a mutant allele and X^B is a normal allele, what were the genotypes of George and Ann's **parents**?

	George's parents	Ann's parents
A	X^BX^b X^BY	X^BX^B X^BY
B	X^BX^B X^bY	X^BX^B X^BY
C	X^BX^b X^BY	X^BX^b X^BY
D	X^BX^B X^bY	X^BX^B X^bY

14. A hybrid is created from a cross between two closely related plants whose chromosome numbers are 14 and 28.

Which of the following statements is true for the offspring of this cross?

A Their cells contain 21 chromosomes and they are fertile.

B Their cells contain 21 chromosomes and they are infertile.

C Their cells contain 42 chromosomes and they are fertile.

D Their cells contain 42 chromosomes and they are infertile.

[Turn over

15. A new species of organism is considered to have evolved when a population

A is isolated from the rest of the population by a geographical barrier

B shows increased variation due to mutations

C can no longer interbreed with the rest of the population

D is subjected to increased selection pressures in its habitat.

16. A plant which has a diploid chromosome number 26 was discovered growing in the vicinity of two different species of the same genus which proved to be its parents. The gametes from one parent plant contained 7 chromosomes. What would be the diploid chromosome number of the other plant?

A 12

B 20

C 33

D 40

17. The dark variety of the peppered moth became common in industrial areas of Britain following the increase in the production of soot during the Industrial Revolution.

The increase in the dark form was due to

A dark moths migrating to areas which gave the best camouflage

B a change in the prey species taken by birds

C an increase in the mutation rate

D a change in selection pressure.

18. Below is a list of statements about osmoregulation in fish.

1 Fresh water fish produce a large volume of dilute urine.

2 Salt water bony fish secrete excess salts at the gills.

3 Salt water bony fish have to drink sea water.

Which of the statements are correct?

A 1, 2 and 3

B 1 and 2 only

C 1 and 3 only

D 2 and 3 only

19. The rate of flow of urine of a salmon in fresh water is given as $5.0\,cm^3$/kg of body mass/hour. The volume of urine produced by a 2·5 kg salmon over a period of 5 hours is

A $12.5\,cm^3$

B $25.0\,cm^3$

C $50.0\,cm^3$

D $62.5\,cm^3$.

20. Various factors are involved in causing water to pass through a plant from the soil to the leaves.

Which of the following describes correctly **two** of these factors?

	The water concentration in the soil is	The water concentration in the xylem of the leaf is
A	greater than in the root hairs	lower than in the mesophyll cells
B	greater than in the root hairs	greater than in the mesophyll cells
C	lower than in the root hairs	lower than in the mesophyll cells
D	lower than in the root hairs	greater than in the mesophyll cells

21. Which line of the table correctly describes the effect of light and dark on the condition of guard cells and stomatal pores of a green plant?

	Light conditions	Stomatal pores	Guard cells
A	dark	closed	turgid
B	dark	open	flaccid
C	light	open	flaccid
D	light	open	turgid

22. The diagram below represents the distribution in the intertidal zone of two species of barnacle, X and Y.

The larvae are free-swimming but become attached to rocks where they develop into fixed adults.

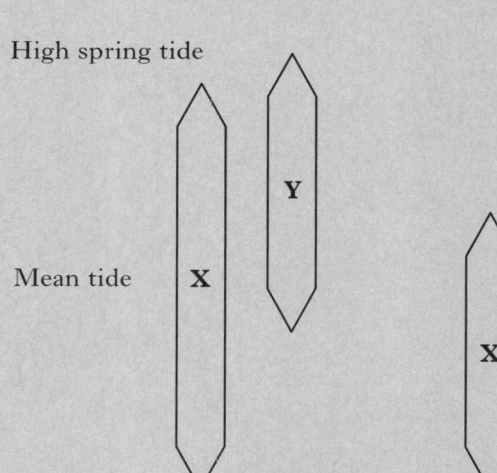

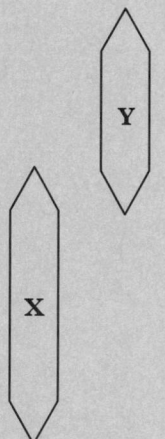

On the basis of the above information, which of the following hypotheses can be made?

A Species X is more tolerant to water loss than species Y.

B There is no competition between the two species.

C Species X is more tolerant of fluctuations in temperature than species Y.

D There is interspecific competition.

23. If a plant has a low compensation point, it may be deduced that

A it requires a high intensity of light for photosynthesis

B it has a high rate of respiration at low intensities of light

C it is able to photosynthesise efficiently at low temperatures

D it is able to photosynthesise efficiently at low intensities of light.

24. The Jacob-Monod model of gene expression involves the following steps.

1 Gene expression
2 Exposure to inducer substances
3 Removal of inhibition
4 Binding to repressor substance

The correct order of these steps is

A 2, 4, 3, 1
B 3, 4, 2, 1
C 4, 1, 2, 3
D 1, 4, 2, 3.

25. The graph shows the growth of an organism over a period of 4 months.

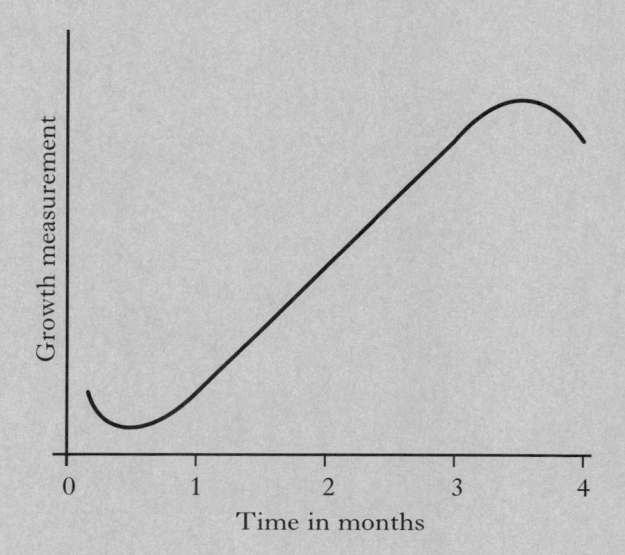

The graph shows changes in the

A mass of an insect
B dry mass of an annual plant
C length of an insect
D length of an annual plant.

[Turn over

26. The following graphs show the relationship between the concentration of the plant growth substance IAA and its promoting or inhibiting effect on the development of certain plant organs.

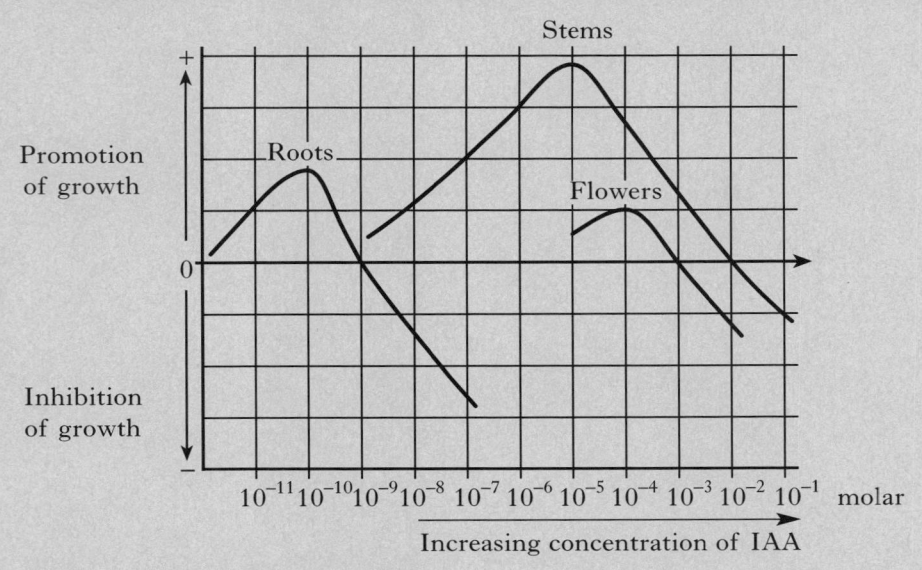

A concentration of 10^{-4} molar solution of IAA will

A promote stem growth but inhibit flower growth

B promote root growth but inhibit stem growth

C promote flower growth and promote stem growth

D inhibit stem growth and inhibit root growth.

---

27. *Xanthium*, a short-day plant, was exposed to different treatments of dark and light. The diagrams indicate the duration, in hours, of these different treatments.

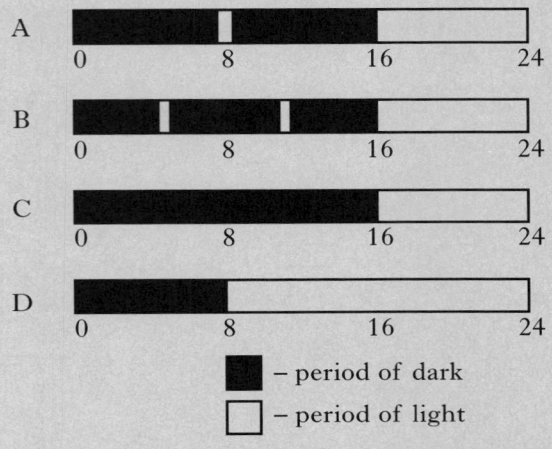

■ – period of dark
□ – period of light

Which of the above treatments would result in flowering?

28. Which of the following is a function of GA (gibberellic acid) but **not** of IAA (indole acetic acid)?

A Breaking of bud dormancy

B Promotion of fruit development

C Stimulation of cell division

D Inhibition of leaf fall

29. During succession in plant communities, a number of changes take place in the ecosystem. Which line of the table correctly describes some of these changes?

	Species diversity	Biomass	Food web complexity
A	rises	rises	rises
B	rises	falls	rises
C	falls	rises	rises
D	rises	rises	falls

30. Which of the following does **not** occur during succession from a pioneer community of plants to a climax community?

A Soil fertility increases.

B Larger plants replace smaller plants.

C An increasing amount of light reaches ground-dwelling plants.

D Each successive community makes the habitat less favourable for itself.

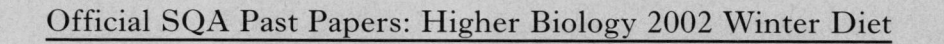

[Turn over for Section B on *Page ten*]

SECTION B

All questions in this section should be attempted.

1. The diagram below represents some of the structures present in an animal cell.

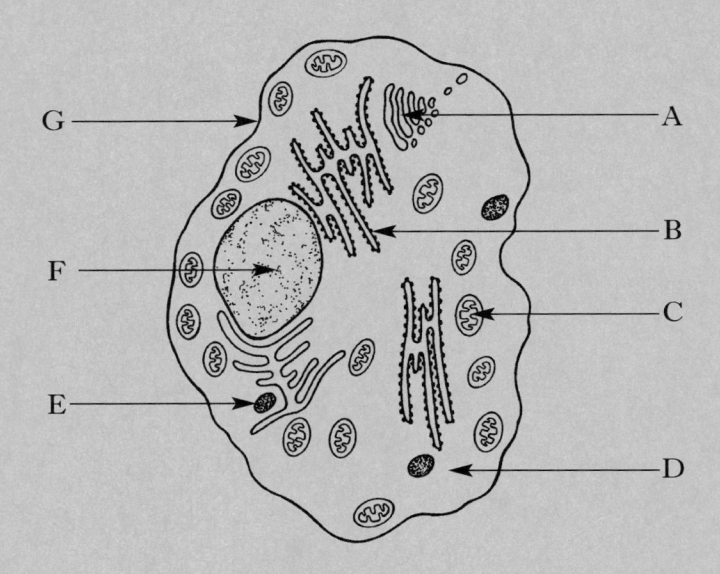

Complete the table by using a letter from the diagram to show which structure carries out each function.

(Each letter may be used **once**, **more than once** or **not at all**.)

Function	Letter
mRNA synthesis	
Translation of mRNA	
Contains enzymes for use in phagocytosis	
Processing and packaging for secretion	
Aerobic ATP production	
Selective ion uptake	

3

2. (a) The graph below shows the effects of increasing carbon dioxide concentration on the rate of photosynthesis at different light intensities and temperatures.

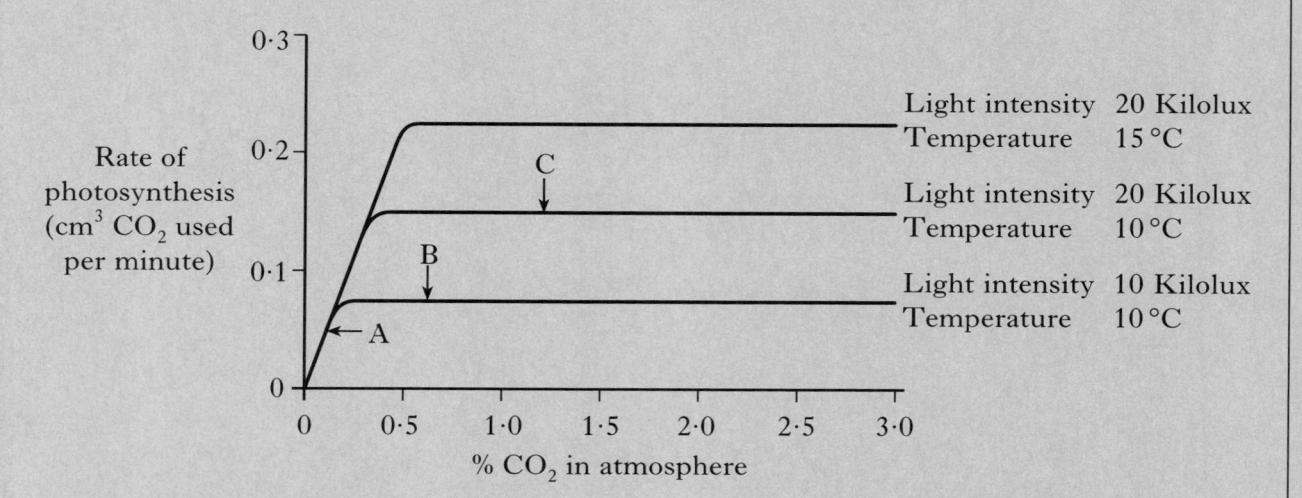

Use the information in the graph to complete the table below.

Tick (✓) **one** box in each row to indicate the factor which is limiting the rate of photosynthesis at points A, B and C.

Graph point	Light intensity	Temperature	Carbon dioxide concentration
A			
B			
C			

2. (continued)

(b) Diagram 1 below shows a leafy shoot. Sugars manufactured in leaf A are transported to other parts of the shoot. Diagram 2 shows the distribution of these sugars 18 hours later.

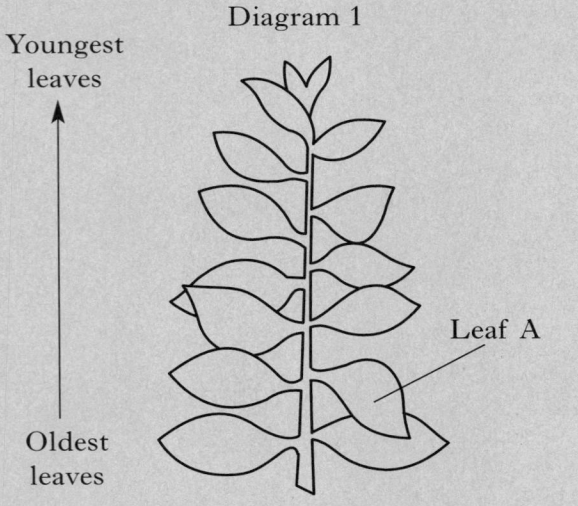

Diagram 1 — Leafy shoot at start

Diagram 2 — Shading shows where sugars made in leaf A were present after 18 hours

From the results, suggest **two** conclusions that can be drawn about the transport of sugars in the leafy shoot over the 18 hour period.

Conclusion 1 _____

Conclusion 2 _____

3. The diagram below represents stages in respiration in yeast.

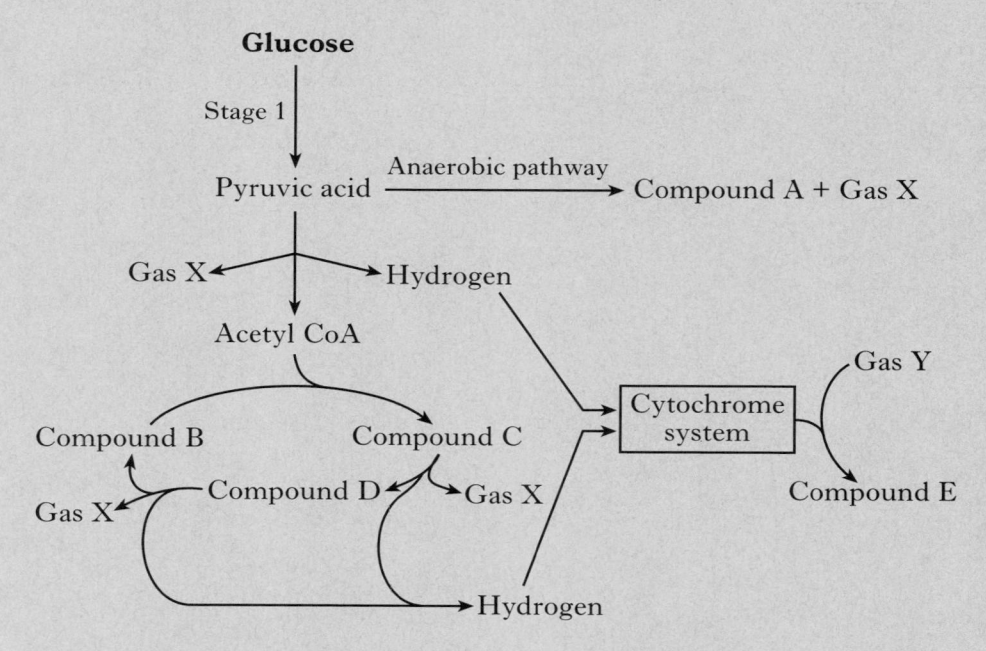

(a) Complete the table below by inserting a letter from the diagram to identify a compound which has the number of carbon atoms shown.

Number of carbon atoms	Compound
6	
4	
2	

(b) Name Stage 1 and state its location in the yeast cell.

Name _____

Location _____

(c) Apart from glucose, name **two** other substances which must be present for Stage 1 to take place.

_____ and _____

(d) (i) Name the carrier which transports hydrogen to the cytochrome system.

_____

(ii) Name gas Y and compound E.

Gas Y _____

Compound E _____

(e) Name a product of aerobic respiration which is **not** shown in the diagram.

_____

4. The diagram below represents replication of part of a DNA molecule.

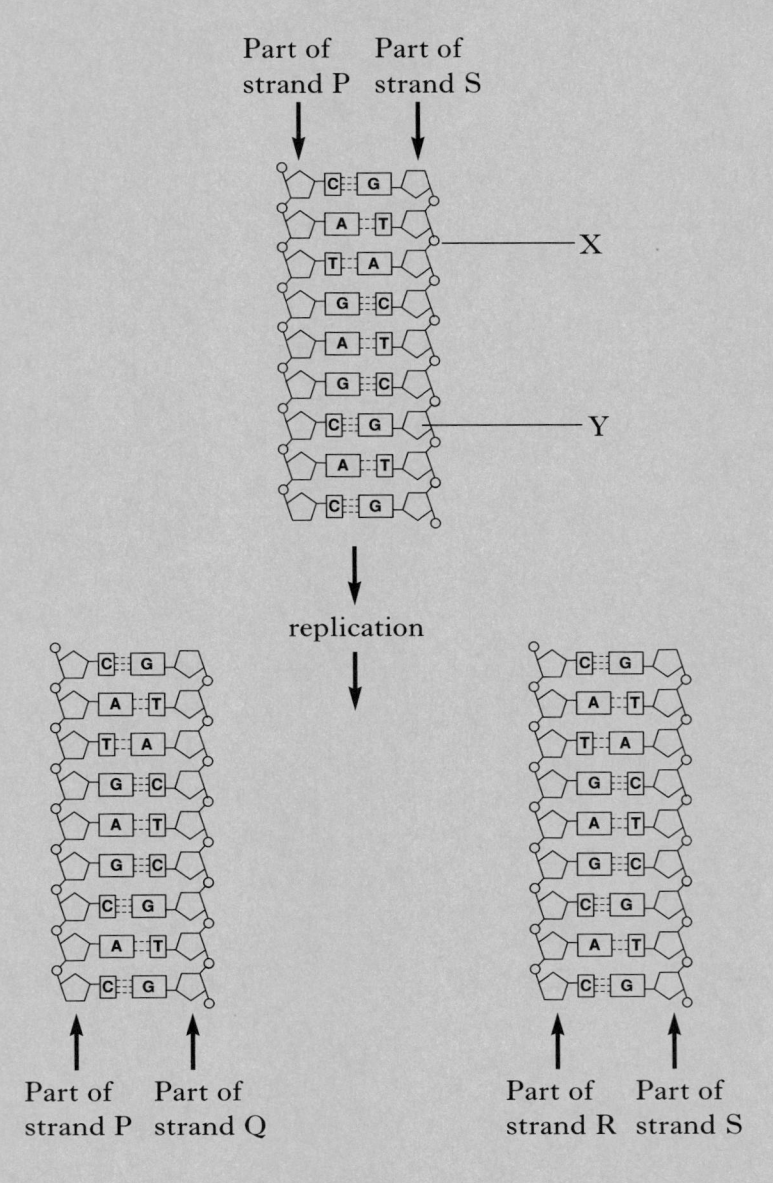

(a) Name the components labelled X and Y on the diagram.

X _____

Y _____

(b) Apart from length, give **one** structural feature of a DNA molecule which is **not** shown in the diagram.

_____

4. (continued)

(c) Name the bonds shown in the diagram which must be broken at the start of replication.

_____ **1**

(d) The full length of DNA strand P has 18% adenine bases and 26% cytosine bases.

(i) Calculate the combined percentage of thymine and guanine bases in strand P.

Space for calculation

Percentage _____ % **1**

(ii) Calculate the percentage of guanine bases in strand S.

Space for calculation

Percentage _____ % **1**

(e) The base sequence of the nucleotides on the part of strand P in the diagram is CATGAGCAC.

(i) Write a possible base sequence for this part of strand P in each of the following mutations.

1 Insertion _____ **1**

2 A single substitution _____ **1**

(ii) Other than chemical substances, name **one** mutagenic agent that can cause such changes to the base sequence of DNA.

_____ **1**

[Turn over

5. The diagram below shows a respirometer which was used to measure the rate of respiration of various living materials. The investigation was carried out at 20 °C.

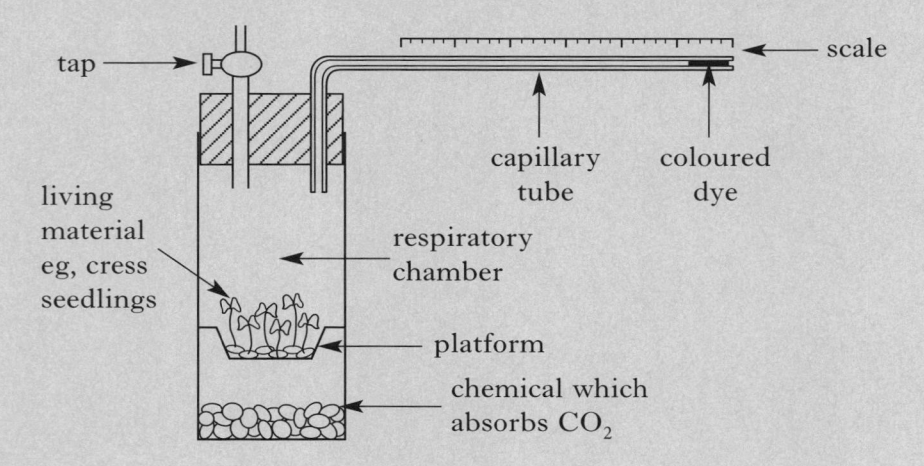

The living material was placed on the platform in the respiratory chamber. The tap was left open for 10 minutes. The tap was then closed and coloured dye was introduced into the end of the capillary tube. The capillary tube had a cross-sectional area of 3 mm². The rate of respiration is expressed as mm³ of oxygen used per gram of living material per minute and can be calculated by using the following formula.

$$\text{Rate of respiration} = \frac{\text{Cross - sectional area of capillary tube (mm}^2\text{)} \times \text{distance moved by coloured dye (mm)} \times 60}{\text{Time taken for the coloured dye to move the distance (s)} \times \text{mass of living material (g)}}$$

The table below shows the results of the investigation.

Living material	Mass of living material (g)	Distance moved by coloured dye (mm)	Time taken (s)	Rate of respiration (mm³ O₂/g/min)
Cress seedlings	30	25	60	2·5
Apple tissue	37·5	25	120	1·0
Fresh liver tissue	60	50	15	10·0
Earthworm	10	15	45	

(a) **Complete the table** by calculating the rate of respiration of an earthworm.
Space for calculation

(b) Different masses of living tissue were used in each experiment.

Explain how the results still allow a valid comparison of the rates of respiration.

5. (continued)

(c) With some living tissue it was found that over a 10 minute period the distance moved by the dye was too little to be measured accurately.

How could the apparatus be modified to overcome this problem?

_____

_____ 1

(d) To improve the reliability of the results for cress seedlings, the experiment was replicated six times. The results are shown in the table below.

Trial	1	2	3	4	5	6
Results ($mm^3 O_2$/g/min)	2·52	2·53	2·48	2·49	0·20	2·51

The results of trial 5 differ from the others. Suggest **one** possible source of error that could account for this result.

_____

_____

_____ 1

(e) The experiment with cress seedlings was carried out in darkness. Explain why the results would have been invalid if the experiment had been carried out in the light.

_____

_____

_____ 2

[Turn over

5. (continued)

(f) In a further investigation the rate of respiration of fresh liver tissue was measured over a range of temperatures. The results are shown in the table below.

Temperature (°C)	10	15	30	35	40	45
Rate of respiration (mm³ O₂/g/min)	2·0	4·0	9·5	13·0	18·5	15·5

Using the **full area** of the grid below, plot a line graph of rate of respiration against temperature.

(Additional graph paper, if required, can be found on page 32.)

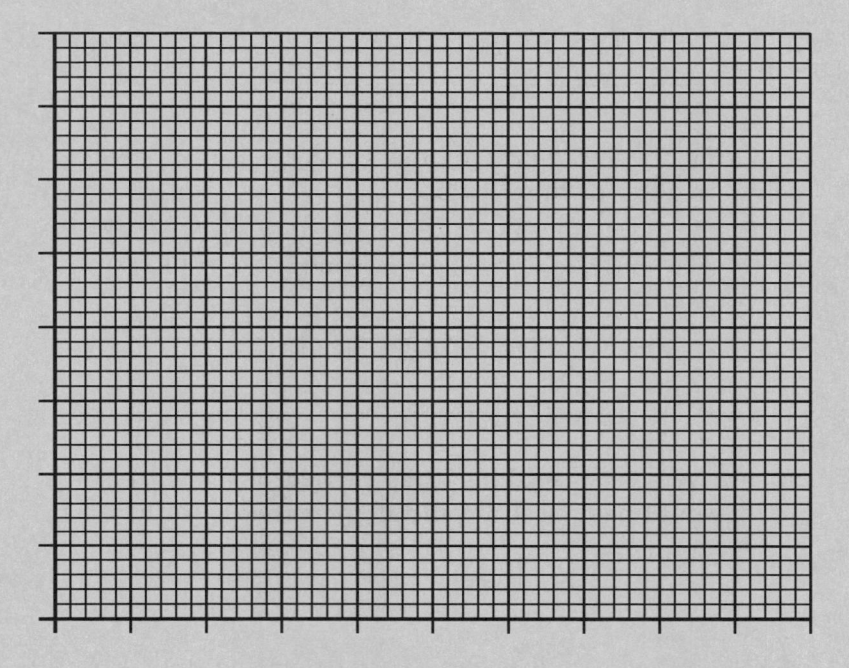

6. (a) The table below shows the characteristics of the leaves of two plant species.

Species	Cuticle	Leaf hairs
Phaseolus	Thin	Absent
Pelargonium	Thick	Present

The graph below compares transpiration from these plants.

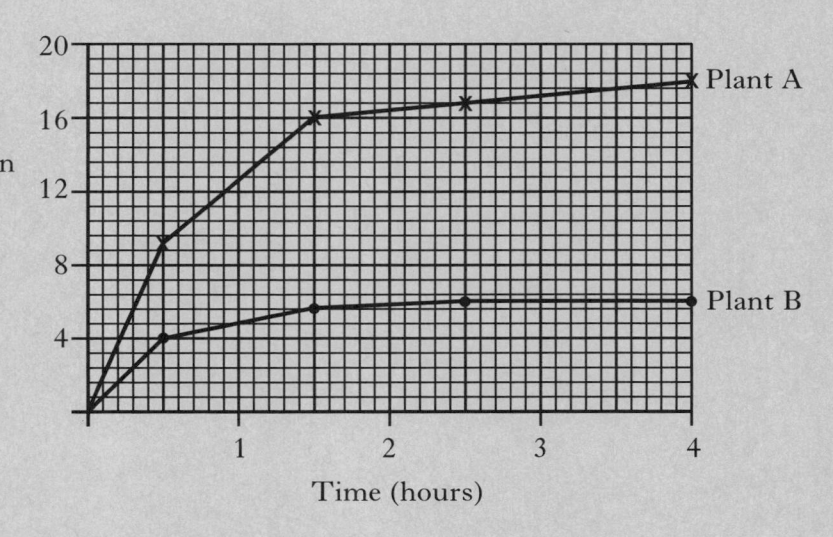

From the graph, identify the plant, A or B which is *Pelargonium* and justify your choice.

Plant _____

Justification _____

_____

_____

(b) Environmental changes have an effect on the rate of transpiration of plants such as *Phaseolus sp* and *Pelargonium sp*.

Complete the table below by using the words **increase**, **decrease** or **no change** to show the effect.

Environmental change	Effect on rate of transpiration
Decreased humidity	
Decreased temperature	
Light to dark	
Increased wind speed	

6. (continued)

(c) The diagram below shows a transverse section through the stem of a hydrophyte.

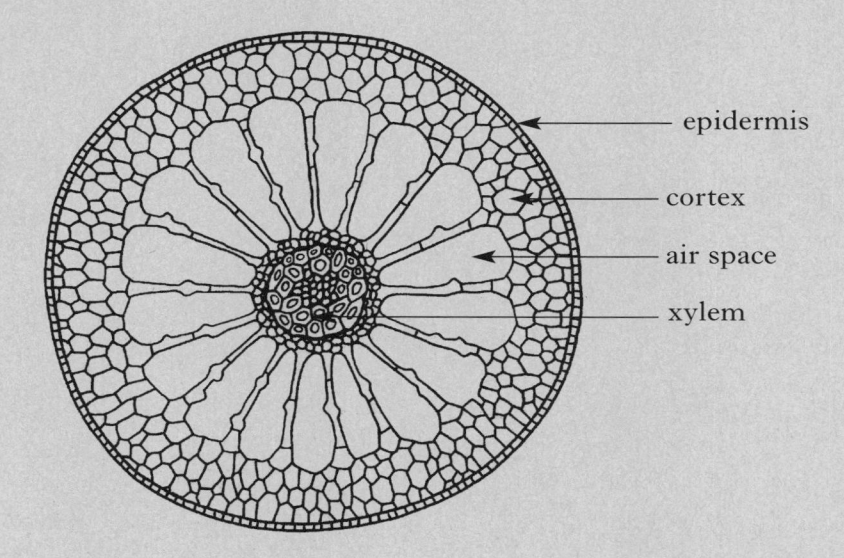

(i) What is the function of the air spaces?

_____

_____ 1

(ii) State the benefit of the xylem tissue being situated at the centre of the stem.

_____

_____ 1

7. The diagram below represents an animal cell which is dividing.

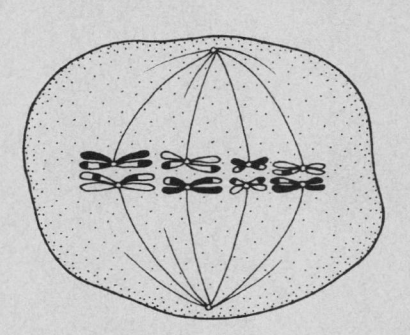

(a) Select **two** features shown in the diagram which show that the cell is dividing by meiosis.

Feature 1 _____

_____

Feature 2 _____

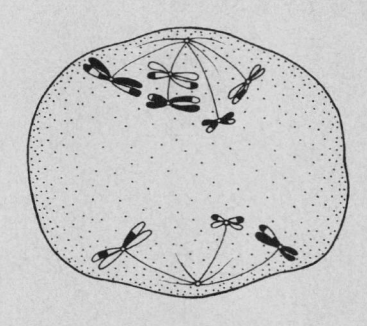

_____

(b) The following diagram shows the same cell at a later stage in meiosis.

(i) What type of chromosome mutation is shown in the diagram?

_____

(ii) State the chromosome numbers which are present in the gametes formed from this cell.

Chromosome numbers _____ and _____

(c) A human liver cell contains 6·0 units of DNA.
How many units of DNA are present in the following human cells?

1 Ovum _____ units

2 Gamete mother cell _____ units

[Turn over

Marks

8. Feather colour in budgerigars is controlled by two genes located on different chromosomes. Each gene has two alleles: A is dominant to a, and B is dominant to b.

Information on genotypes and their associated phenotypes is shown in the table below.

Genotypes	*Phenotypes*
AAbb, Aabb	yellow
aaBB, aaBb	blue
aabb	white
Alleles A and B both present	green

A male of genotype aaBb was crossed with a female of genotype AaBb.

(*a*) State the phenotype of each bird.

male ______________________________ female ______________________________ **1**

(*b*) Complete the table below by:

1 inserting the genotypes of the male and female gametes **1**

2 showing the possible genotypes of the offspring. **1**

<table>
<tr><td colspan="2" rowspan="2">Gametes</td><td colspan="4">Female</td></tr>
<tr><td></td><td></td><td></td><td></td></tr>
<tr><td rowspan="2">Male</td><td></td><td></td><td></td><td></td><td></td></tr>
<tr><td></td><td></td><td></td><td></td><td></td></tr>
</table>

(*c*) In the spaces below, show the expected phenotype ratio of the offspring.

_________ green : _________ blue : _________ yellow : _________ white **1**

9. The diagram below shows a transverse section through the stem of a tree that was cut down in November 2001.

(a) **Insert an X** within the annual ring that was formed in 1999.

(b) One of the annual rings is much narrower than the others.
Explain how heavy infestation by leaf-eating caterpillars may account for this observation.

(c) Describe **one** way in which the structure of a spring xylem vessel differs from that of a summer xylem vessel.

(d) Name the meristem that is responsible for the formation of the new cells that differentiate into xylem vessels.

(e) How can the control of cell differentiation be explained in terms of gene activity?

[Turn over

10. The graph below shows changes in the α-amylase concentration and the starch content of a barley grain during early growth and development.

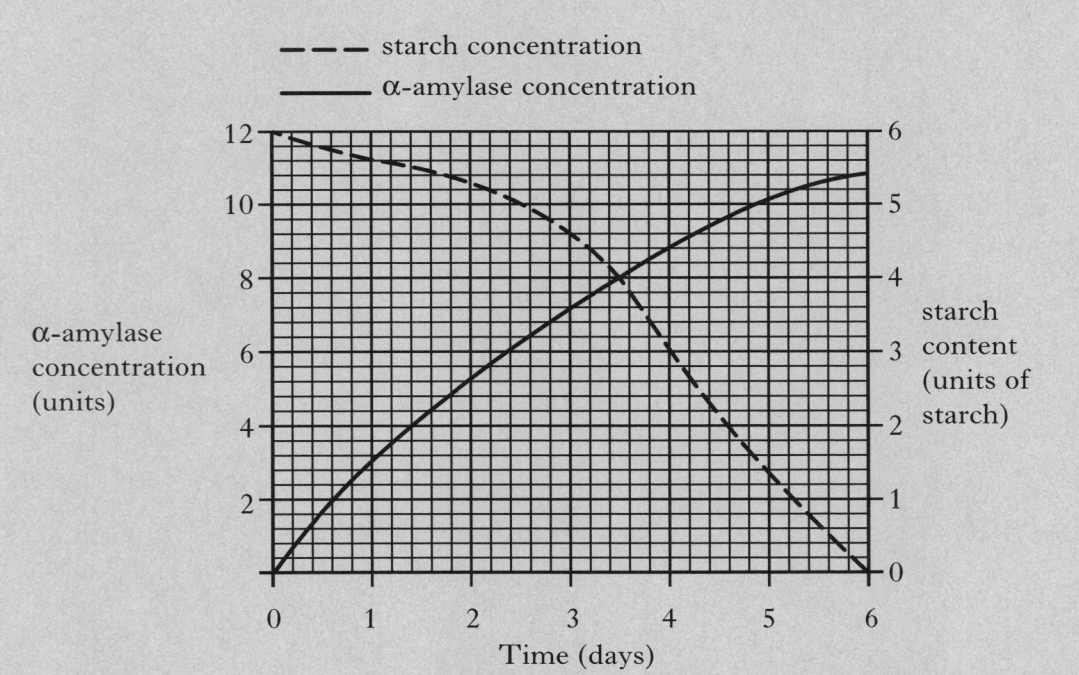

- - - starch concentration
——— α-amylase concentration

(a) (i) After how many days is the starch content of the barley grains decreased by 50%?

_____

(ii) Account for the increasing rate of breakdown of starch as shown in the graph.

_____

_____

(b) In which tissue of the barley grain is α-amylase synthesised?

_____

(c) Name the following.

1 The plant growth substance that initiates the synthesis of α-amylase

_____

2 The site of production of this plant growth substance within the barley grain

_____

11. The diagram below outlines the role of a gland and three hormones which influence growth and development in humans.

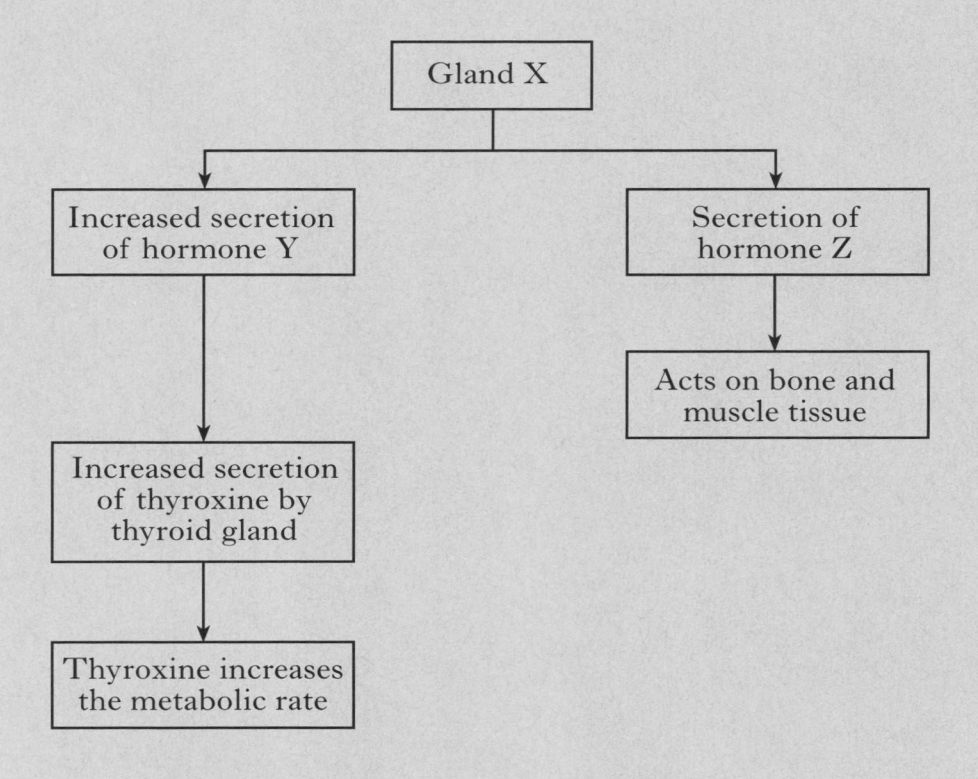

```
                    Gland X
                   /       \
                  ↓         ↓
        Increased secretion    Secretion of
        of hormone Y           hormone Z
                  ↓                 ↓
        Increased secretion    Acts on bone and
        of thyroxine by        muscle tissue
        thyroid gland
                  ↓
        Thyroxine increases
        the metabolic rate
```

(a) Name gland X and hormones Y and Z.

Gland X _____

Hormone Y _____ Hormone Z _____   2

(b) The control of thyroxine secretion is an example of negative feedback control. Given this information, predict the effect of an increase in thyroxine on gland X.

_____

_____   1

(c) Name a chemical element and a vitamin needed for the growth and development of bone.

Chemical element _____

Vitamin _____   1

[Turn over

12. Plants require the chemical elements nitrogen, phosphorus, magnesium and potassium for normal growth and development.

The boxes below refer to:

1. the appearance of plants that results from deficiencies in these elements
2. the importance of these elements in normal growth and development of plants.

A	B	C
Leaf bases appear red	Overall growth of the plant is reduced	Roots show increased growth in length
D	E	F
Leaves are chlorotic	Essential in the formation of chlorophyll	Essential for membrane transport
G	H	I
Essential in the formation of ATP	Essential in the formation of DNA and RNA	Essential for the synthesis of proteins

(a) Which **two** boxes would describe the appearance of plants which were grown in soil deficient in phosphorus?

Letters _____ and _____

(b) Which **three** boxes give reasons why nitrogen is essential for normal growth and development in plants?

Letters _____ , _____ and _____

(c) A deficiency in different elements can result in the same abnormal growth and development.

Name **two** elements which, if deficient, cause leaves to appear chlorotic (box D).

Elements _____ and _____

(d) Give an account of the link between boxes B and H.

_____

_____

_____

13. The table below shows the relationship between the concentration of lead in the placenta and the average birth mass of human babies.

Range of concentration of lead in placenta (units)	Average birth mass (kg)
25 – 29	2·32
20 – 24	2·87
15 – 19	3·40
10 – 14	3·74
5 – 9	4·40

(a) (i) Describe the relationship between the concentration of placental lead and average birth mass.

(ii) State the effect of lead on cell functions.

(b) (i) Describe the effect of thalidomide on fetal development.

(ii) Name **two** drugs which have the effect of causing a decrease in the expected birth weight.

Drug 1 _____ Drug 2 _____

[Turn over

14. During pharmaceutical trials for a new medicine, a healthy subject volunteered to drink 1 litre of water.

Samples of urine were taken over a 3 hour period as it flowed from the kidney to the bladder.

These samples were used to determine the rate of urine production and the salt concentration of the urine.

The results are shown in Graph 1 below.

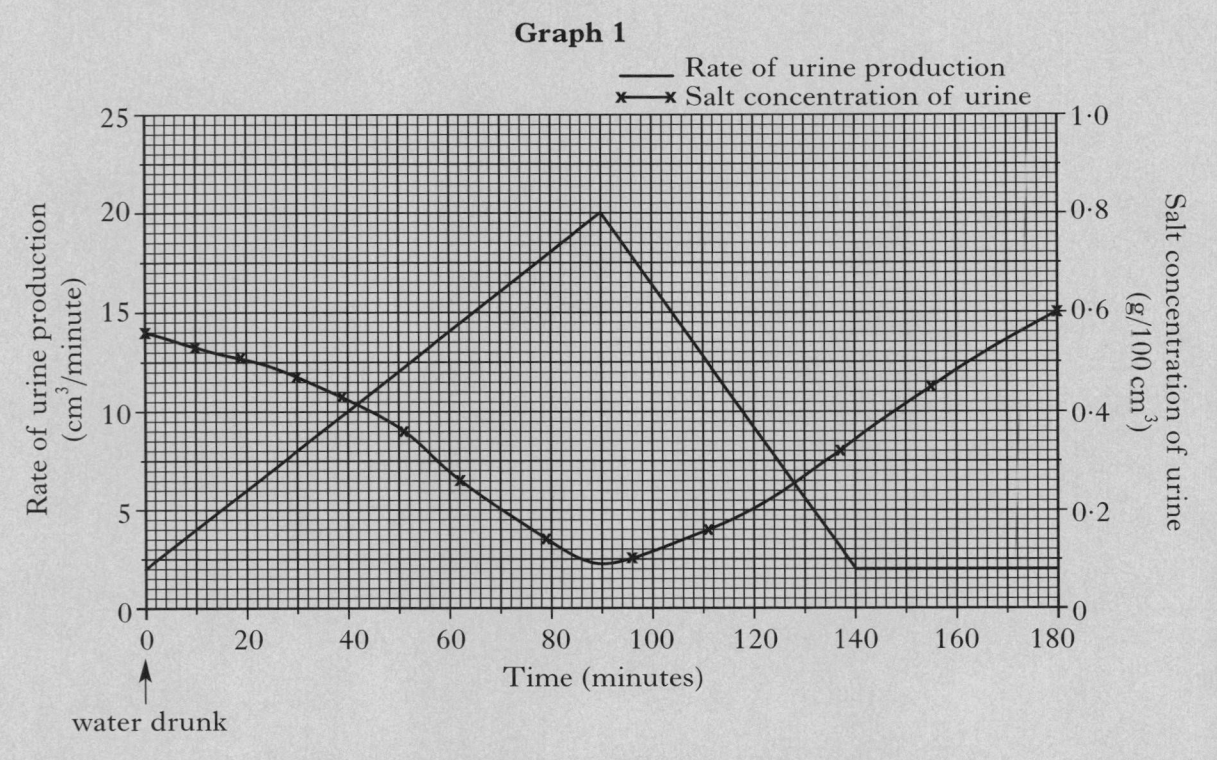

Graph 1

(a) From **Graph 1**, how long did it take, after drinking the water, for the rate of urine production to return to the initial value?

Time _____ minutes

(b) From **Graph 1**, describe the relationship between the rate of urine production and salt concentration in the urine over the 3 hour period.

_____

_____

_____

_____

(c) From **Graph 1**, calculate the decrease in the salt concentration of the urine over the first 90 minutes.

Space for calculation

_____ g/100 cm³

14. (continued)

In a further investigation, 10 mg of the medicine was administered to the volunteer who then drank 1 litre of water.

The results are shown in **Graph 2**.

Graph 2

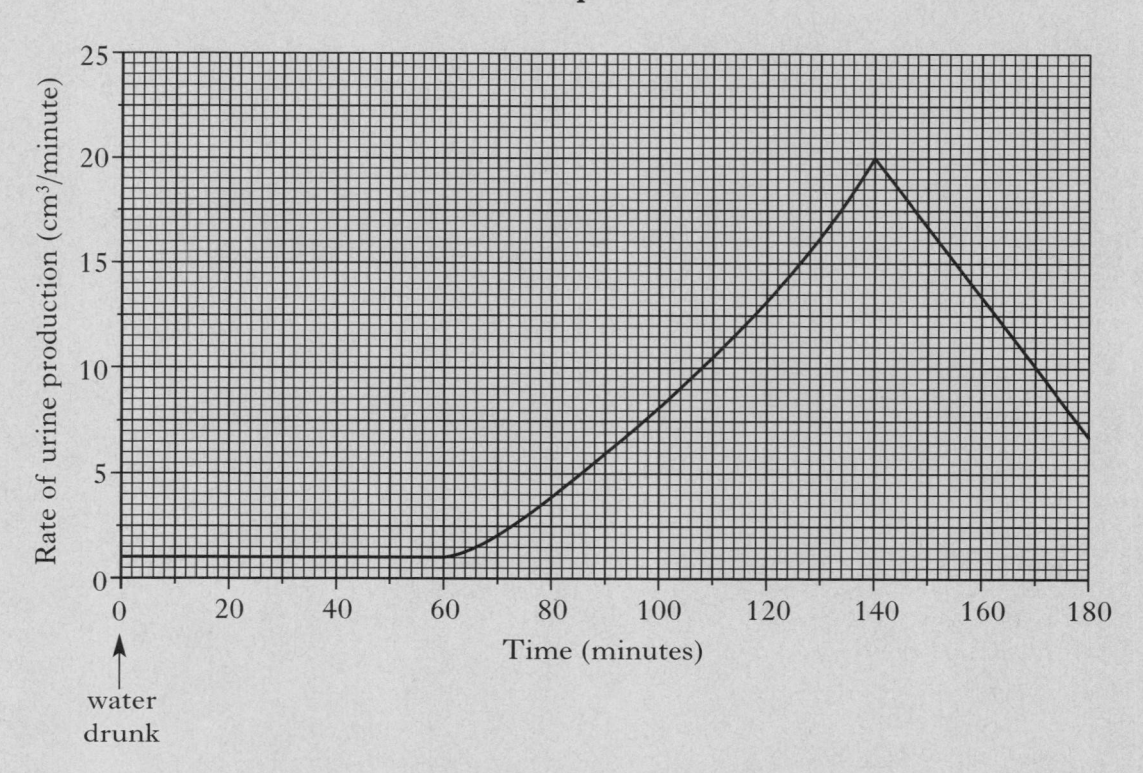

[Graph showing Rate of urine production (cm³/minute) vs Time (minutes). Water drunk at time 0. Rate stays at ~1 cm³/minute from 0 to 60 minutes, then rises to peak of 20 cm³/minute at 140 minutes, then falls to ~7 cm³/minute at 180 minutes.]

(d) From **Graphs 1** and **2**, calculate the difference between the rates of production of urine 90 minutes after the start.

Space for calculation

_____ cm³/minute   **1**

(e) From **Graphs 1** and **2**, explain how the evidence supports the statement that the medicine affects the rate of water reabsorption in the kidney.

_____

_____

_____   **2**

(f) Predict how the result of the trial may have differed if 20 mg of the medicine had been administered.

_____

_____   **1**

15. Various factors have an effect on the size of a population.

The flowchart outlines how population density may be regulated.

Population increases above the optimum → Increased effect of density-dependent factors → Population decreases

Optimum population supported by the environment

Return to optimum population supported by the environment

Population decreases below the optimum → Decreased effect of density-dependent factors → Population increases

(a) Competition for food between members of the same species has a density-dependent effect on a population. What term describes competition between members of the same species?

_____ 1

(b) Other than competition for food between members of the same species, name **two** other density-dependent factors that affect population size and explain how each factor has its effect.

1 Factor _____

Explanation of effect _____

_____

_____ 1

2 Factor _____

Explanation of effect _____

_____

_____ 1

SECTION C

Both questions in this section should be attempted.

Note that each question contains a choice.

Questions 1 and 2 should be attempted on the blank pages which follow.

Supplementary sheets, if required, may be obtained from the invigilator.

Labelled diagrams may be used where appropriate.

Marks

1. Answer **either** A **or** B.

   A. Write notes on each of the following:

   (i) photosynthetic pigments;   5

   (ii) the light-dependent stage of photosynthesis.   5

   OR   (10)

   B. Write notes on each of the following:

   (i) invasion of cells by viruses and the production of more viruses;   5

   (ii) cellular defence mechanisms in animals.   5

      (10)

In question 2, ONE mark is available for coherence and ONE mark is available for relevance.

2. Answer **either** A **or** B.

   A. Give an account of the importance of the physiological and behavioural adaptations shown by the desert rat in water conservation.   (10)

   OR

   B. Give an account of artificial selection with reference to selective breeding and somatic fusion.   (10)

[END OF QUESTION PAPER]

[Turn over

SPACE FOR ANSWERS

ADDITIONAL GRAPH PAPER FOR QUESTION 5(*f*)

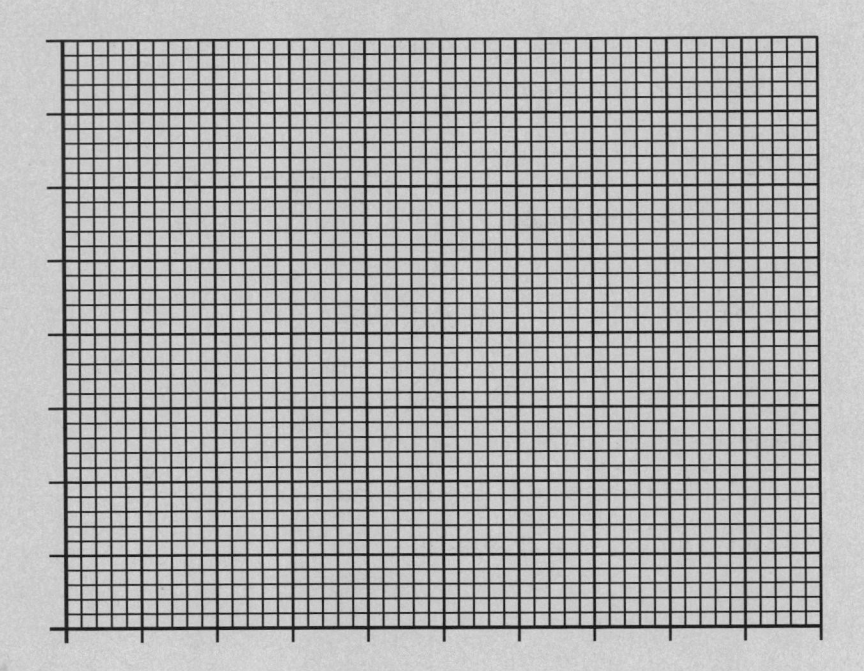

Official SQA Past Papers: Higher Biology 2003

FOR OFFICIAL USE

X007/301

Total for Sections B and C

NATIONAL QUALIFICATIONS 2003

MONDAY, 26 MAY 1.00 PM – 3.30 PM

BIOLOGY HIGHER

Fill in these boxes and read what is printed below.

Full name of centre

Town

Forename(s)

Surname

Date of birth
Day Month Year   Scottish candidate number   Number of seat

SECTION A—Questions 1–30 (30 marks)

Instructions for completion of Section A are given on page two.

SECTIONS B AND C (100 marks)

1 (a) All questions should be attempted.
   (b) It should be noted that in **Section C** questions 1 and 2 each contain a choice.

2 The questions may be answered in any order but all answers are to be written in the spaces provided in this answer book, and must be written clearly and legibly in ink.

3 Additional space for answers and rough work will be found at the end of the book. If further space is required, supplementary sheets may be obtained from the invigilator and should be inserted inside the **front** cover of this book.

4 The numbers of questions must be clearly inserted with any answers written in the additional space.

5 Rough work, if any should be necessary, should be written in this book and then scored through when the fair copy has been written.

6 Before leaving the examination room you must give this book to the invigilator. If you do not, you may lose all the marks for this paper.

SCOTTISH QUALIFICATIONS AUTHORITY

LIB X007/301 6/13020

SECTION A

Read carefully

1. Check that the answer sheet provided is for Biology Higher (Section A).
2. Fill in the details required on the answer sheet.
3. In this section a question is answered by indicating the choice A, B, C or D by a stroke made in **ink** in the appropriate place in the answer sheet—see the sample question below.
4. For each question there is only **one** correct answer.
5. Rough working, if required, should be done only on this question paper—or on the rough working sheet provided—**not** on the answer sheet.
6. At the end of the examination the answer sheet for Section A **must** be placed inside the front cover of this answer book.

Sample Question

The apparatus used to determine the energy stored in a foodstuff is a

A respirometer
B calorimeter
C klinostat
D gas burette.

The correct answer is **B**—calorimeter. A **heavy** vertical line should be drawn joining the two dots in the appropriate box in the column headed **B** as shown in the example on the answer sheet.

If, after you have recorded your answer, you decide that you have made an error and wish to make a change, you should cancel the original answer and put a vertical stroke in the box you now consider to be correct. Thus, if you want to change an answer D to an answer B, your answer sheet would look like this:

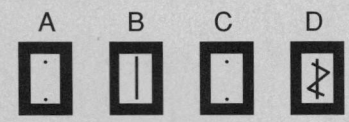

If you want to change back to an answer which has already been scored out, you should enter a tick (✓) to the **right** of the box of your choice, thus:

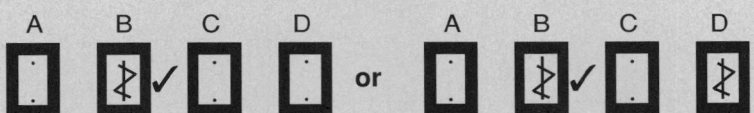

SECTION A

All questions in this section should be attempted.

Answers should be given on the separate answer sheet provided.

1. The table below shows the concentrations of three ions found in sea water and in the sap of the cells of a seaweed.

	Ion concentrations (mg l^{-1})		
	potassium	sodium	chloride
sea water	0·01	0·55	0·61
cell sap	0·57	0·04	0·60

Which of the following statements is supported by the data in the table?

A Potassium and sodium ions are taken into the cell by active transport.

B Potassium and chloride ions are removed from the cell by diffusion.

C Sodium ions are removed from the cell by active transport.

D Chloride and sodium ions are removed from the cell by diffusion.

2. A piece of muscle was cut into three strips, X, Y and Z, and treated as described in the table.

Their final lengths were then measured.

Muscle strip	Solution added to muscle	Muscle length (mm)	
		Start	After 10 minutes
X	1% glucose	50	50
Y	1% ATP	50	45
Z	1% ATP boiled and cooled	50	46

From the data it may be deduced that

A ATP is not an enzyme

B muscles contain many mitochondria

C muscles synthesise ATP in the absence of glucose

D muscles do not use glucose as a source of energy.

3. DNA controls the activities of a cell by coding for the production of

A proteins

B carbohydrates

C amino acids

D bases.

4. The diagram below shows part of a DNA molecule during replication. Bases are represented by numbers and letters.

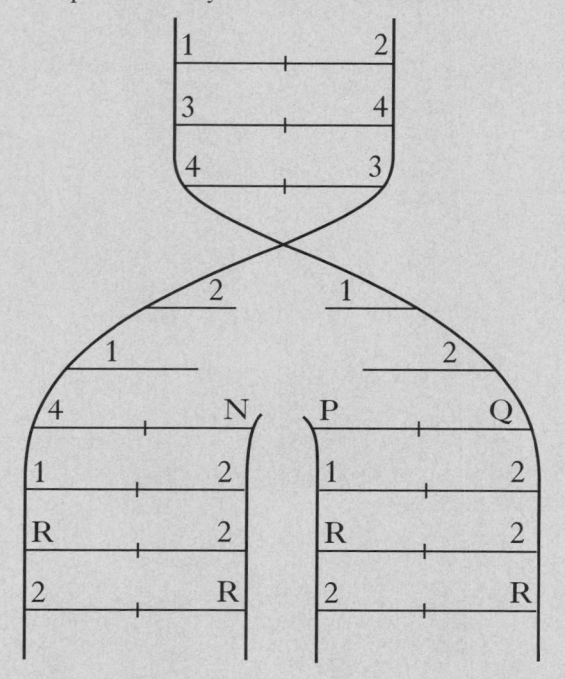

If 1 represents adenine and 3 represents cytosine, which line in the table identifies correctly the bases represented by the letters N, P, Q and R?

	N	P	Q	R
A	guanine	cytosine	guanine	thymine
B	cytosine	guanine	cytosine	adenine
C	guanine	cytosine	cytosine	adenine
D	cytosine	guanine	guanine	adenine

[Turn over

5. The table below contains statements which may be TRUE or FALSE concerning DNA replication and mRNA synthesis.

   Which line in the table is correct?

	Statement	DNA replication	mRNA synthesis
A	Occurs in the nucleus	TRUE	FALSE
B	Involved in protein synthesis	TRUE	TRUE
C	Requires free nucleotides	TRUE	FALSE
D	Involves complementary base pairing	TRUE	TRUE

6. A fragment of DNA was found to have 60 guanine bases and 30 adenine bases. What is the total number of deoxyribose sugar molecules in this fragment?

   A 30

   B 45

   C 90

   D 180

7. The diagram represents part of a molecule of DNA on which a molecule of RNA is being synthesised.

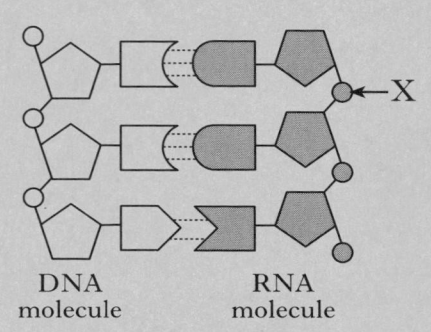

   What does component X represent?

   A Ribose sugar

   B Deoxyribose sugar

   C Phosphate

   D Ribose phosphate

8. The sequence of triplets on a strand of DNA is shown below.

   ATTACACCGTACCAATAG

   During translation of mRNA made from the above sequence, how many of the tRNA anticodons will have at least one uracil base?

   A 3

   B 4

   C 5

   D 7

9. The function of tRNA in cell metabolism is to

   A transport amino acids to be used in synthesis

   B carry codons to the ribosomes

   C synthesise proteins

   D transcribe the DNA code.

10. Which of the following identifies correctly the sequence in which organelles become involved in the production of an enzyme for secretion?

    A Nucleus → Ribosomes → Golgi Apparatus → Rough ER

    B Ribosomes → Vesicles → Rough ER → Golgi Apparatus

    C Nucleus → Rough ER → Vesicles → Ribosomes

    D Ribosomes → Rough ER → Golgi Apparatus → Vesicles

11. In a pea plant, the alleles for plant height and petal colour are located on separate chromosomes. The dominant alleles are for tallness and pink petals; the corresponding recessive alleles are for dwarfness and white petals. A heterozygous plant was crossed with a plant recessive for both characteristics. If 320 progeny resulted, what would be the predicted number of tall, white plants?

    A 20

    B 60

    C 80

    D 180

12. The relative positions of the genes M, N, O and P on a chromosome were determined by the analysis of percentage recombination. The results are shown in the table.

Genes	Percentage recombination
M and O	5
N and O	16
N and P	8
M and P	19

The correct order of genes on the chromosomes is

A O M P N

B O M N P

C M O N P

D M N O P.

13. The base sequence of a short piece of DNA is shown below.

A G C T T A C G

During replication, an inversion mutation occurred on the complementary strand synthesised on this piece of DNA.

Which of the following is the mutated complementary strand?

A T C G A A T G A

B A G C T T A G C

C T C G A A T C G

D T C G A A T G C

14. In a diploid organism with the genotype HhMmNNKK, how many genetically distinct types of gamete would be produced?

A 2

B 4

C 8

D 16

15. Scientists visiting a group of four islands, P, Q, R and S, found similar spiders on each island. They carried out tests to see if the spiders from different islands would interbreed.

The results are summarised in the table below.

(✓ indicates successful interbreeding. ✗ indicates that fertile young were not produced.)

		Spiders from			
		P	Q	R	S
Spiders from	P	✓	✓	✗	✗
	Q	✓	✓	✗	✗
	R	✗	✗	✓	✗
	S	✗	✗	✗	✓

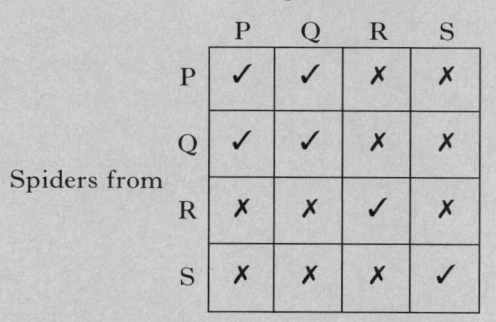

How many species of spider were present on the four islands?

A One

B Two

C Three

D Four

16. In sexual reproduction, which of the following is **not** a source of genetic variation?

A Non-disjunction

B Linkage

C Mutation

D Crossing over

17. Which of the following statements regarding polyploidy is correct?

A It is more common in animals than in plants.

B It is the term used to describe the four haploid cells formed at the end of meiosis.

C It can produce individuals with increased vigour.

D It always results from non-disjunction of chromosomes.

[Turn over

18. In genetic engineering, endonucleases are used to

A join fragments of DNA together

B cut DNA molecules into fragments

C close plasmid rings

D remove cell walls for somatic fusion.

19. Which of the following is a plant response to invasion by a foreign organism?

A Increased production of tannin

B Engulfing of invaders by specialised cells

C Production of antibodies

D Closing of stomata

20. Which of the following adaptations allows a plant to tolerate grazing by herbivores?

A Thick waxy cuticle

B Leaves reduced to spines

C Low meristems

D Thorny stems

Question 21 is at the top of the next column

21. In which of the following do **both** adaptations reduce the rate of water loss from a plant?

A Thin cuticle and rolled leaf

B Rolled leaf and sunken stomata

C Sunken stomata and large surface area

D Thin cuticle and needle-shaped leaves

22. The diagram below shows a transverse section through a plant stem.

In which region would cambium cells be found?

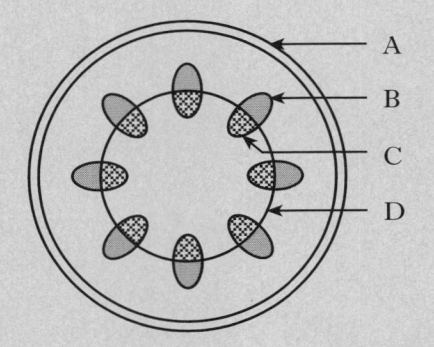

23. The graph below shows the blood glucose concentrations of two women before and after each swallowed 50 g of glucose.

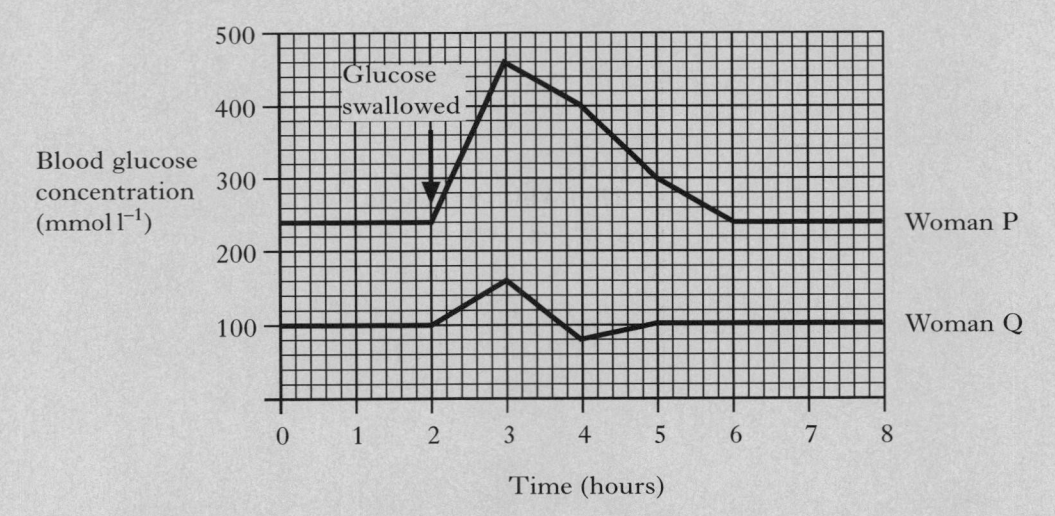

When did the rate of change of blood glucose concentration of the two women differ most?

A Between hours 2 and 3

B Between hours 3 and 4

C Between hours 4 and 5

D Between hours 5 and 6

24. During the germination of barley grains, the plant growth substance GA (Gibberellic Acid) promotes the synthesis of the enzyme α-amylase in the

A aleurone layer

B endosperm

C embryo

D cotyledon.

25. Which of the following statements about the plant growth substances IAA (Indole Acetic Acid) and GA (Gibberellic Acid) is correct?

A An increase in IAA content of a leaf promotes leaf abscission.

B A decrease in IAA content of a leaf promotes leaf abscission.

C An increase in GA content of a leaf promotes leaf abscission.

D A decrease in GA content of a leaf promotes leaf abscission.

26. Which line in the table below identifies correctly the sites of production of the hormones ADH and glucagon?

	ADH	Glucagon
A	Pituitary gland	Liver
B	Kidney	Liver
C	Kidney	Pancreas
D	Pituitary gland	Pancreas

27. Which one of the following factors that can limit rabbit population size is density independent?

A Viral disease

B The population of foxes

C The biomass of the grass

D High rainfall

28. Which of the following best defines "population density"?

A The number of individuals present per unit area of a habitat

B The number of individual organisms present in a habitat

C A group of individuals of the same species which make up part of an ecosystem

D The maximum number of individuals which the resources of the environment can support

29. Which of the following does **not** occur during succession from a pioneer community of plants to a climax community?

A Soil fertility increases.

B Larger plants replace smaller plants.

C An increasing intensity of light reaches ground-dwelling plants.

D Each successive community makes the habitat less favourable for itself.

30. Dietary deficiency of vitamin D causes rickets. This effect is due to

A poor uptake of phosphate into growing bones

B poor calcium absorption from the intestine

C low vitamin D content in the bones

D loss of calcium from the bones.

Candidates are reminded that the answer sheet MUST be returned INSIDE the front cover of this answer book.

[Turn over

SECTION B

All questions in this section should be attempted.

1. (a) The diagram below represents cells in the lining of the small intestine of a mammal.

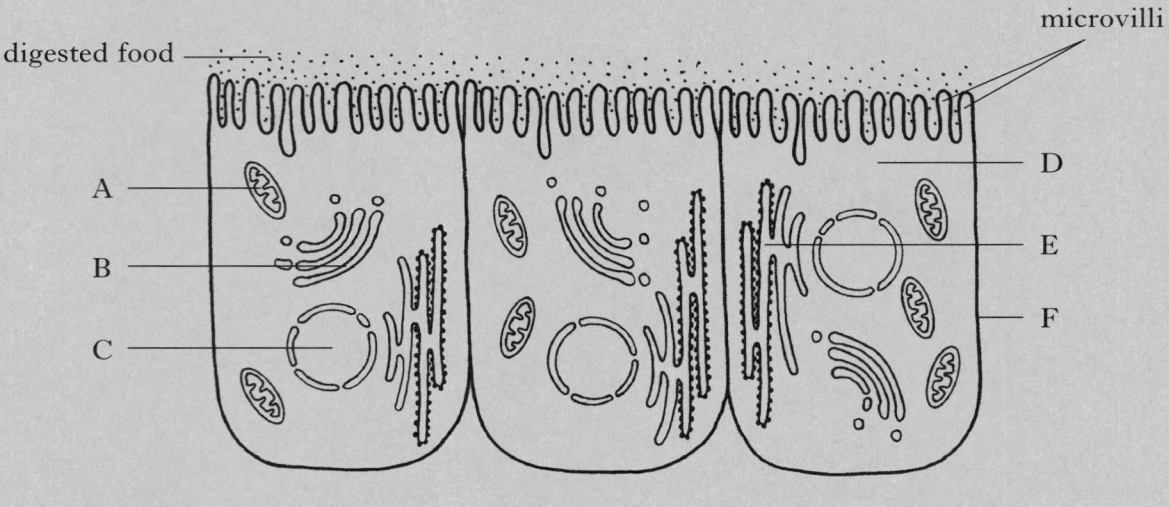

(i) The table below gives information about organelles shown in the diagram.

Complete the table by inserting the appropriate letters, names and functions.

Letter	Name of organelle	Function
E	Rough endoplasmic reticulum	
		Site of aerobic respiration
B	Golgi apparatus	
		Site of mRNA synthesis

(ii) Suggest a reason for the presence of microvilli in this type of cell.

1. (continued)

(b) The diagram below summarises the process of photosynthesis in a chloroplast.

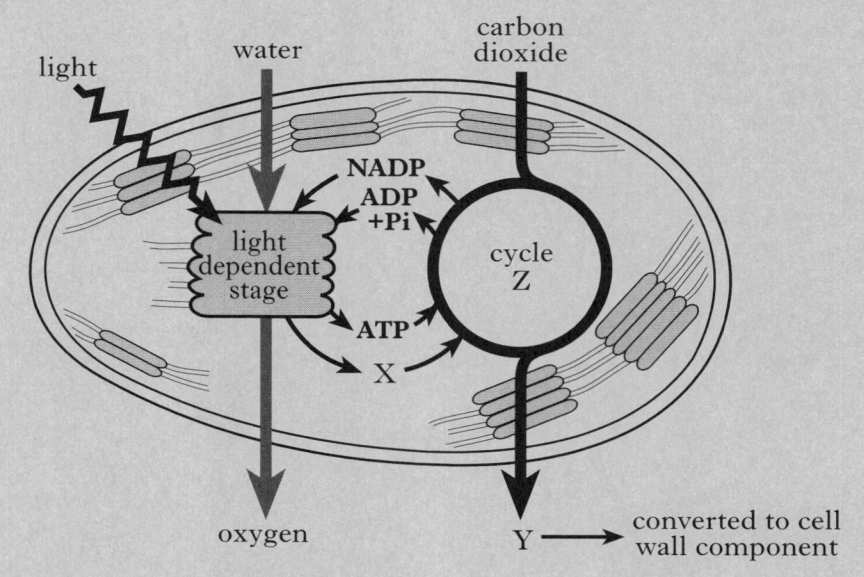

(i) Name molecules X and Y.

X _____

Y _____   1

(ii) State the exact location of the light dependent stage within a chloroplast.

_____   1

(iii) Name cycle Z.

_____   1

(iv) Name the cell wall component referred to in the diagram.

_____   1

[Turn over

2. An investigation was carried out to compare photosynthesis in oak and nettle leaves.

Six discs were cut from each type of leaf and placed in syringes containing a solution that provided carbon dioxide. A procedure was used to remove air from the leaf discs to make them sink. The apparatus was placed in a darkened room. The discs were then illuminated with a lamp covered with a green filter. Leaf discs which carried out photosynthesis floated.

The positions of the discs one hour later are shown in the diagram below.

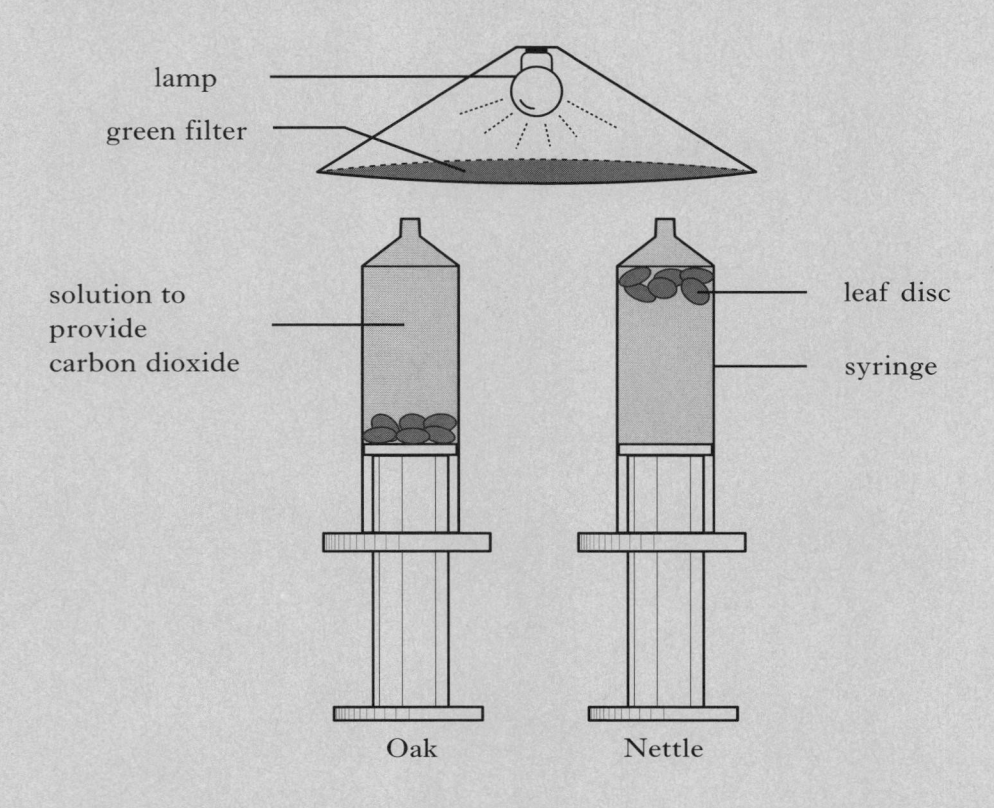

(a) Suggest a reason why the investigation was carried out in a darkened room.

_____

_____ 1

(b) Explain why it was good experimental procedure to use six discs from each plant.

_____

_____

_____ 1

2. (continued)

(c) In setting up the investigation, precautions were taken to ensure that the results obtained would be valid.

Give **one** precaution relating to the preparation of the leaf discs and **one** precaution relating to the solution that provided carbon dioxide.

Leaf discs _____

_____ 1

Solution that provided carbon dioxide _____

_____ 1

(d) Suggest a reason why the leaf discs which carried out photosynthesis floated.

_____ 1

(e) Nettles are shade plants which grow beneath sun plants such as oak trees.

Explain how the results show that nettles are well adapted as shade plants.

_____

_____

_____ 2

(f) What name is given to the light intensity at which the carbon dioxide uptake for photosynthesis is equal to the carbon dioxide output from respiration?

_____ 1

[Turn over

2. **(continued)**

(g) In another investigation, the rate of photosynthesis by nettle leaf discs was measured at different light intensities. The results are shown in the table.

Light intensity (kilolux)	Rate of photosynthesis by nettle leaf discs (units)
10	2
20	26
30	58
40	89
50	92
60	92

Plot a line graph to show the rate of photosynthesis by nettle leaf discs at different light intensities. Use appropriate scales to fill most of the graph paper.
(Additional graph paper, if required, can be found on page 32.)

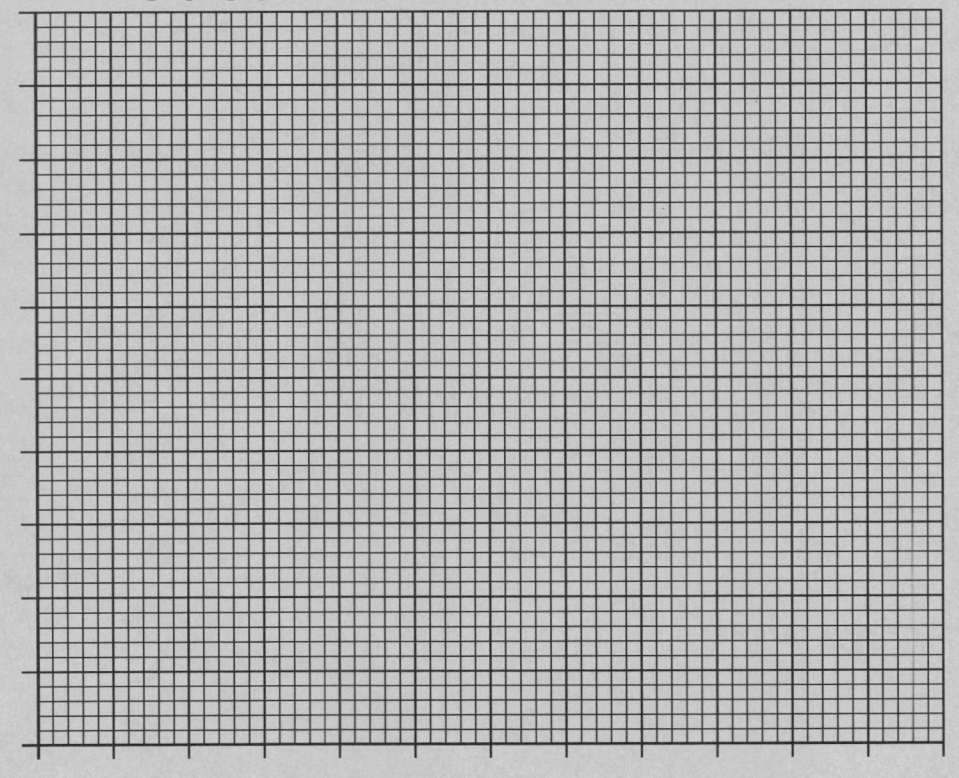

(h) From the table, predict how the rate of photosynthesis at a light intensity of 50 kilolux could be affected by an increase in carbon dioxide concentration. Justify your answer.

Effect on the rate of photosynthesis _____

Justification _____

3. The stages shown below take place when a human cell is invaded by an influenza virus.

Stage 1	Viral nucleic acid enters host cell
Stage 2	
Stage 3	Viral nucleic acid replicates
Stage 4	Synthesis of viral coats
Stage 5	
Stage 6	Rupture of cell and release of viruses

(a) Describe the processes that occur during Stages 2 and 5.

Stage 2 _____

_____

Stage 5 _____

_____

(b) Name the cell organelle at which the viral coats are synthesised during Stage 4.

_____

(c) During a viral infection, a type of white blood cell is stimulated to make antibodies which inactivate the viruses.

(i) Name this type of white blood cell.

_____

(ii) What feature of viruses stimulates these cells to make antibodies?

_____

(iii) New strains of influenza virus appear regularly. Suggest why antibodies produced against one strain of virus are not effective against another strain.

_____

_____

4. An outline of the process of respiration is shown in the diagram below.

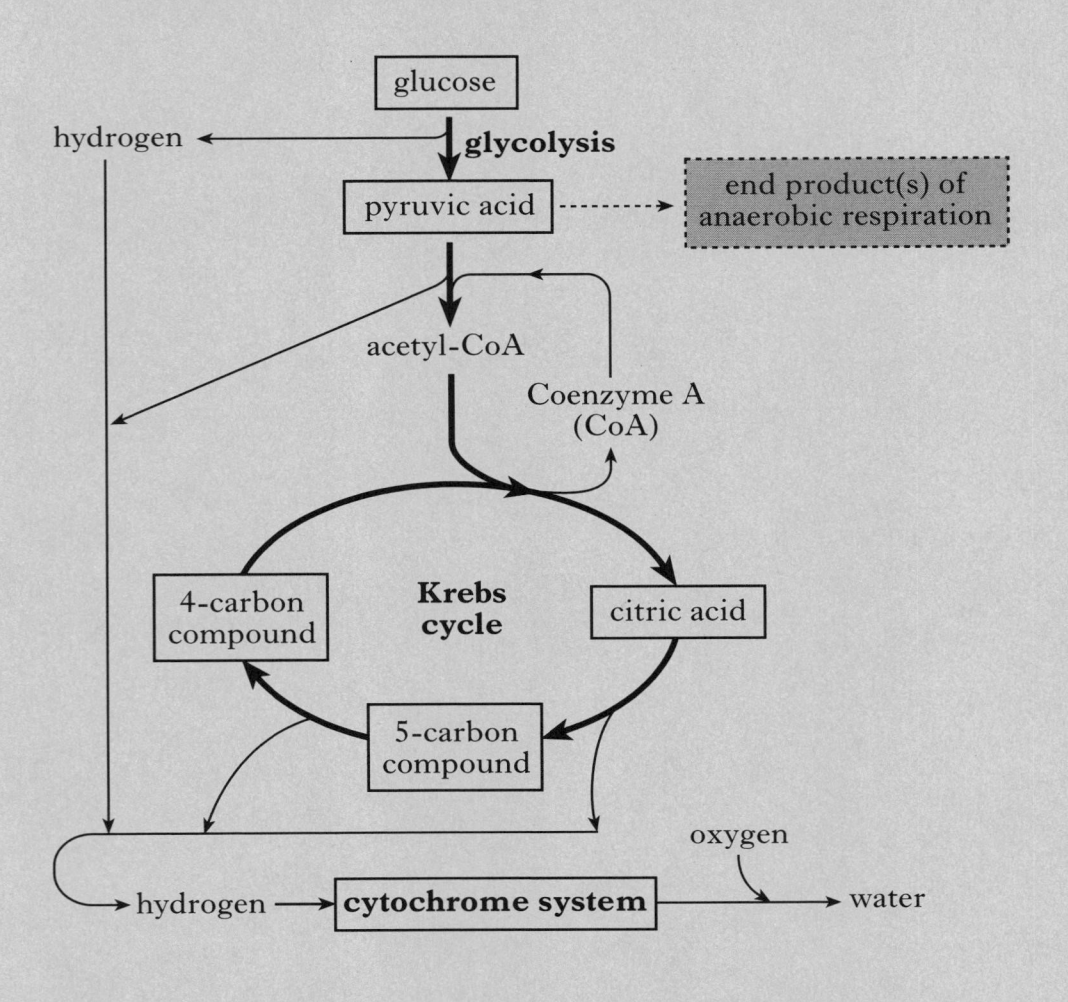

(a) Apart from glucose and enzymes, what chemical substance is essential for glycolysis to occur?

_____ 1

(b) Name the end-product(s) of anaerobic respiration in an animal cell and a plant cell.

(i) Animal cell _____ 1

(ii) Plant cell _____ 1

(c) Name the carrier that transfers hydrogen to the cytochrome system.

_____ 1

4. (continued)

(d) Explain why the cytochrome system cannot function in anaerobic conditions.

_____

_____

_____ **1**

(e) The energy content of glucose is 2900 kJ mol^{-1} and during aerobic respiration 1178 kJ mol^{-1} of this energy is stored in ATP.

Calculate the percentage of the energy content of glucose that is stored in ATP.

Space for calculation

_____ % **1**

(f) Which stage of respiration releases **most** energy for use by the cell?

_____ **1**

[Turn over

5. The diagram below represents a stage of meiosis in a cell from a female fruit fly, *Drosophila*.

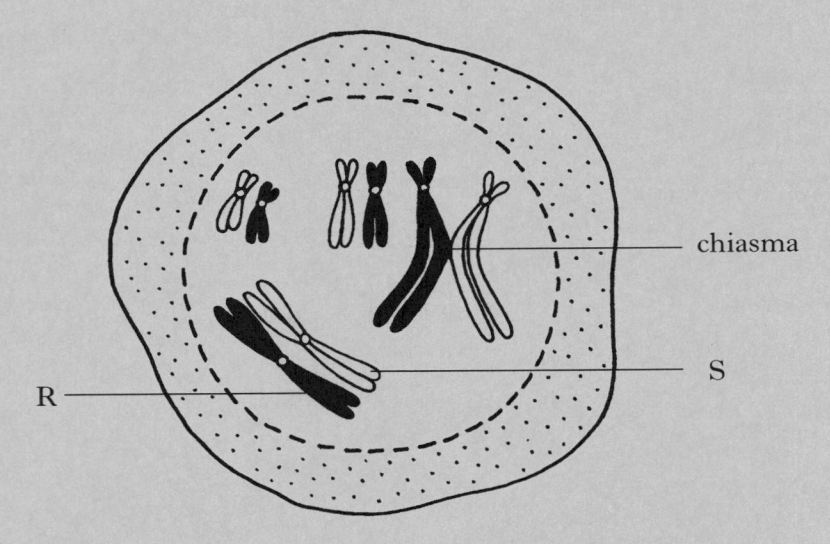

(a) Name the tissue from which this cell was taken.

_____

(b) What is the haploid number of this species?

_____

(c) Chromosomes R and S are homologous. Apart from their appearance, state **one** similarity between homologous chromosomes.

_____

_____

(d) Explain the importance of chiasmata formation.

_____

_____

6. In humans, the allele for red-green colour deficiency (b) is sex-linked and recessive to the normal allele (B).

The family tree diagram below shows how the condition was inherited.

☐ Male without the condition
■ Male with the condition
○ Female without the condition
● Female with the condition

(a) Give the genotypes of individuals S and T.

(i) S _____

(ii) T _____

(b) If individuals Q and R have a son, what is the chance that he will inherit the condition?

Space for calculation

Chance _____

(c) Explain why individual R has the condition although her mother was unaffected.

_____

_____

[Turn over

7. Hawaii is a group of islands isolated in the Pacific Ocean.

Different species of Honeycreeper birds live on these islands.

The heads of four species of Honeycreeper are shown below.

(a) (i) Explain how the information given about Honeycreeper species supports the statement that they occupy different niches.

_____

_____ 1

(ii) What further information would be needed about the four species of Honeycreeper to conclude that they had evolved by adaptive radiation?

_____

_____ 1

(b) The Honeycreeper species have evolved in geographical isolation.

Name **one** other type of isolating barrier involved in the evolution of new species.

_____ 1

8. The marine worm *Sabella* lives in a tube made out of sand grains from which it projects a fan of tentacles for feeding.

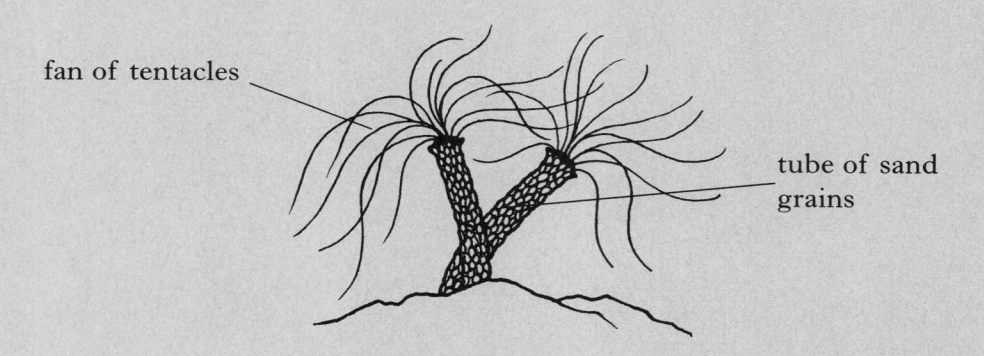

(a) If the worm is disturbed, the fan is immediately withdrawn into the tube. The fan re-emerges a few minutes later.

   (i) Name the type of behaviour illustrated by the withdrawal response.

   _____ 1

   (ii) What is the advantage to the worm of withdrawing its tentacles in response to a disturbance?

   _____
   _____ 1

(b) If a harmless stimulus occurs repeatedly, the withdrawal response eventually ceases.

   (i) Name the type of behaviour illustrated by this modified response.

   _____ 1

   (ii) What is the advantage to the worm of this modified response?

   _____
   _____ 1

[Turn over

9. Limpets (*Patella*) feed by grazing on algae growing on rocks at the seashore.

Graph 1 below shows the effects of limpet population density on the average shell length and total biomass.

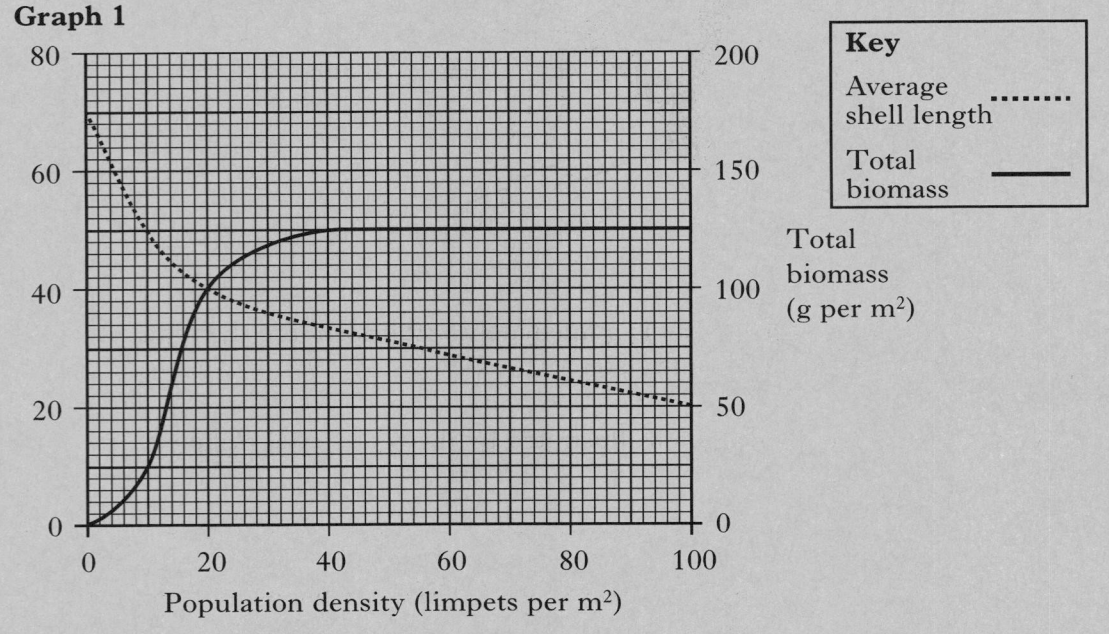

Graph 1

(a) What is the total biomass at a population density of 10 limpets per m²?

_____ g per m²

(b) Identify the population density range (limpets per m²) in which the total biomass increases most rapidly.

Tick the correct box.

0–10 ☐   10–20 ☐   20–30 ☐   30–40 ☐   40–50 ☐

(c) Calculate the average mass of one limpet when the population density is 20 per m².

Space for calculation

Average mass _____ g

(d) Use values from Graph 1 to describe the effect of increasing population density on the total biomass of limpets.

_____

_____

_____

9. (continued)

(e) Explain how intraspecific competition causes the trend in average shell length shown in Graph 1.

_____

_____   **1**

(f) The table below shows information about limpets on shore A which is sheltered and on shore B which is exposed to strong wave action.

Graph 2 below shows the effect of wave action on limpet shell index.

Limpet shell index = $\dfrac{\text{shell height}}{\text{shell length}}$

Shore A (sheltered)		Shore B (exposed)	
Shell height (mm)	Shell length (mm)	Shell height (mm)	Shell length (mm)
16	52	9	21
19	54	11	26
20	55	14	31
21	56	16	34
22	57	17	35
23	58	17	36
26	60	–	–
Average = 21	Average =	Average = 14	Average =

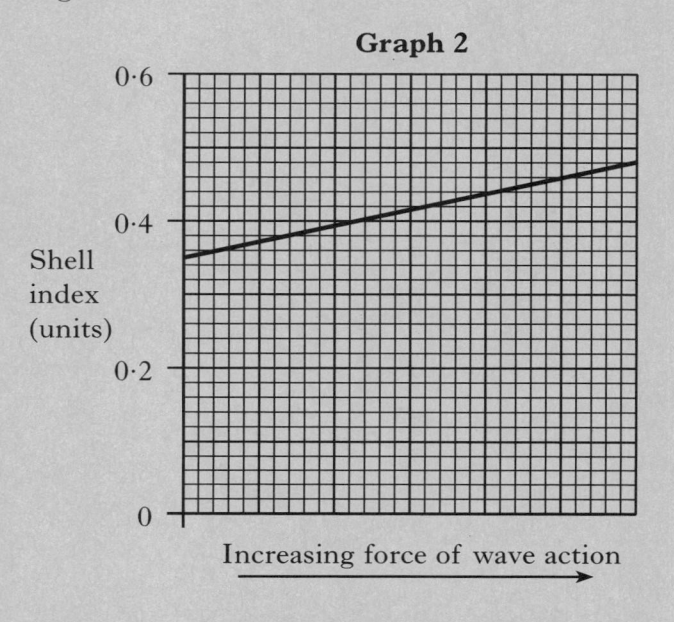

Graph 2

Shell index (units) vs Increasing force of wave action

(i) **Complete the table** by calculating the average shell length of limpets on both shores.

Space for calculation

1

(ii) Express as the **simplest whole number ratio** the average shell height for shore A and shore B.

Space for calculation

Ratio _____ : _____   **1**

(iii) A limpet shell collected on one of the shores had a length of 43 mm and a height of 20 mm. Use Graph 2 to identify which shore it came from and justify your choice.

Tick (✓) the correct box   Shore A ☐   Shore B ☐

Justification _____

_____

_____   **1**

10. (a) The grid below shows adaptations of bony fish for osmoregulation.

A	few, small glomeruli	B	active secretion of salts by gills	C	high filtration rate in kidney
D	active uptake of salts by gills	E	low filtration rate in kidney	F	many, large glomeruli

Use letters from the grid to answer the following questions.

(i) Which **three** adaptations would be found in freshwater fish?

Letters _____ , _____ and _____ .

(ii) Which **two** adaptations would result in the production of a small volume of urine?

Letters _____ and _____ .

(b) The table shows some adaptations of a desert mammal which help to conserve water.

For each adaptation, tick (✓) the correct box to show whether it is behavioural **or** physiological.

Adaptation	Behavioural	Physiological
High level of blood ADH		
Lives in underground burrow		
Nocturnal foraging		
Absence of sweating		

11. (a) The diagram below shows a section through part of a root.

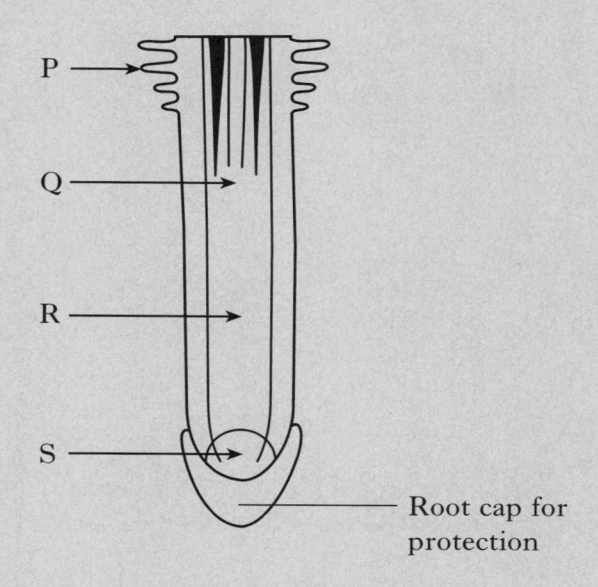

(i) Which letter shows the position of a meristem?

Letter _____

(ii) Name a cell process responsible for increase in length of a root.

_____

(b) The diagram below shows the growth pattern of a locust.

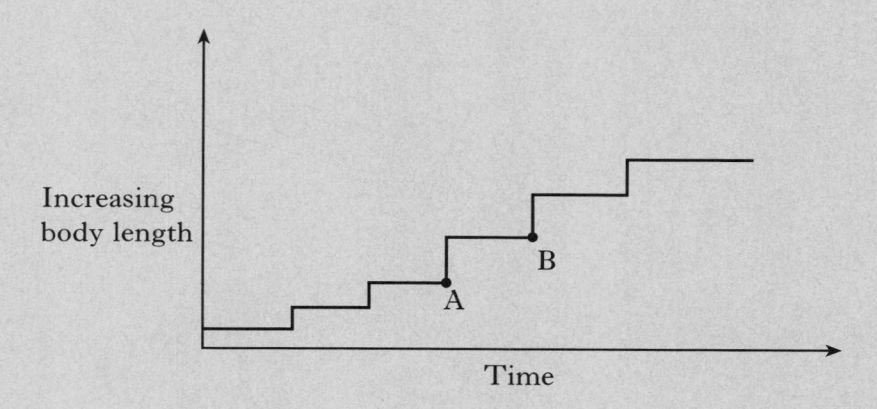

Explain the reason for the shape of the growth pattern between A and B.

_____
_____
_____

12. The diagram below shows the apparatus used to investigate the growth of oat seedlings in water culture solutions. Each solution lacks one element required for normal growth.

The containers were painted black to prevent algal growth.

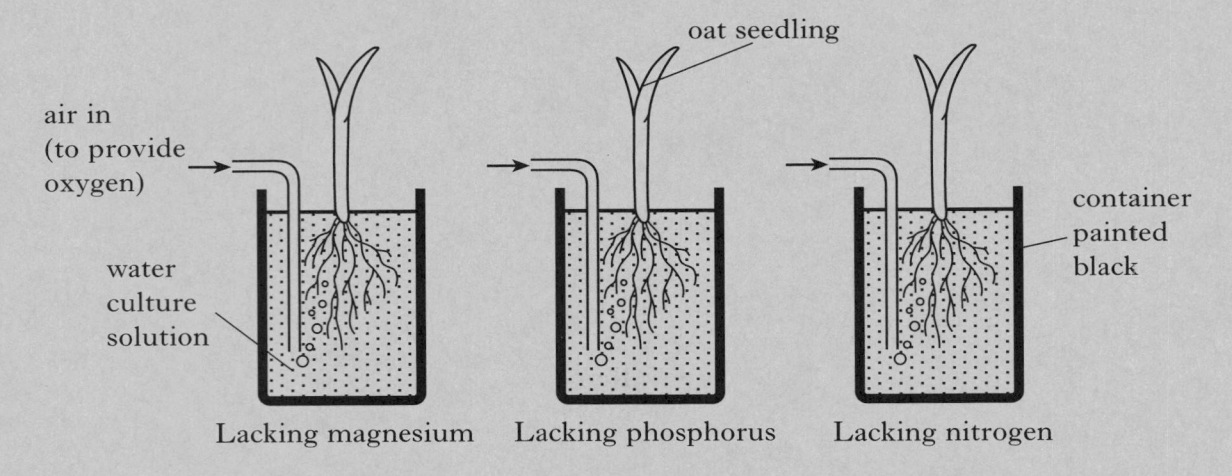

(a) Describe a suitable control for this experiment.

_____

_____

_____ **1**

(b) Suggest a reason why algal growth should be prevented in the culture solutions during the investigation.

_____

_____

_____ **1**

(c) The table below shows the elements investigated and symptoms of their deficiency.

Place ticks (✓) in the correct boxes to match each element with the symptoms of its deficiency.

Element	Symptoms of deficiency	
	Leaf bases red	Chlorotic leaves
Magnesium		
Phosphorus		
Nitrogen		

2

12. (continued)

(d) Name a magnesium containing molecule found in oat seedlings.

(e) Explain why the uptake of elements by oat seedling roots is dependent on the availability of oxygen.

13. The production of thyroxine in mammals is controlled by the hormone TSH. Thyroxine controls metabolic rate in body cells and has a negative feedback effect on gland X.

The diagram below shows the relationship between TSH and thyroxine production.

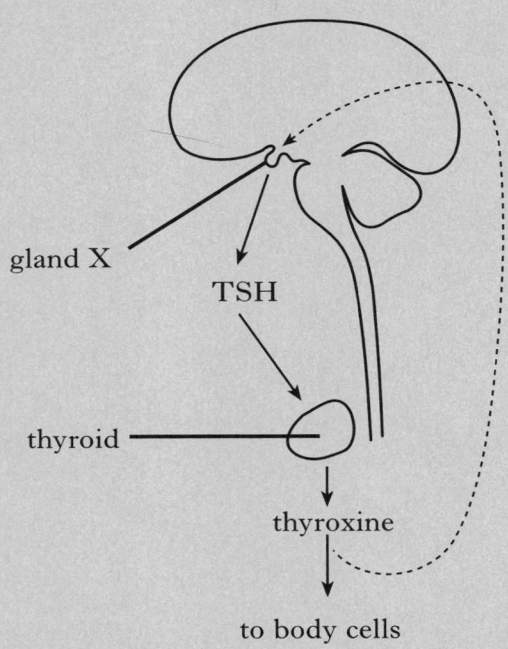

(a) Name gland X.

(b) In an investigation into the effect of thyroxine, groups of rats of similar mass were treated as follows.

Group A were fed a normal diet.
Group B were fed a normal diet plus thyroxine.
Group C were fed a normal diet plus an inhibitor of thyroxine production.

The table below shows the average hourly oxygen consumption in cm³ per gram of body mass in rats from each group.

Group	Average hourly oxygen consumption (cm³g⁻¹)
A	1·6
B	2·8
C	1·2

(i) Explain how the results in the table support the statement that an increase in metabolic rate leads to an increase in oxygen consumption.

13. **(b) (continued)**

(ii) What evidence suggests that rats fed a normal diet make thyroxine?

_____

_____ **1**

(iii) How would the level of TSH production in group A compare with group C?

_____

_____ **1**

(iv) Calculate the percentage decrease in oxygen consumption which results from feeding the thyroxine inhibitor to rats.

Space for calculation

_____ % decrease **1**

(v) The table below relates to aspects of the appearance and behaviour of rats in groups B and C.

Group	Appearance of ears and feet	Behaviour
B	Pink	Lie stretched out
C	Pale	Lie curled up with feet tucked in

Complete the following sentences by underlining **one** of the alternatives in each pair.

1 Compared with rats in group B, the rats in group C have a $\begin{Bmatrix} \text{lower} \\ \text{higher} \end{Bmatrix}$ metabolic rate and show $\begin{Bmatrix} \text{dilation} \\ \text{constriction} \end{Bmatrix}$ of skin blood vessels. **1**

2 The behaviour of rats in group C allows them to $\begin{Bmatrix} \text{lose} \\ \text{conserve} \end{Bmatrix}$ body heat. **1**

[Turn over

SECTION C

Both questions in this section should be attempted.

Note that each question contains a choice.

Questions 1 and 2 should be attempted on the blank pages which follow.

Supplementary sheets, if required, may be obtained from the invigilator.

Labelled diagrams may be used where appropriate.

1. Answer **either** A **or** B.

   A. Give an account of gene mutation under the following headings:

   (i) the occurrence of mutant alleles and the effect of mutagenic agents; **3**

   (ii) types of gene mutation and how they alter amino acid sequences. **7**

   (10)

   OR

   B. Give an account of water movement through plants under the following headings:

   (i) the transpiration stream; **8**

   (ii) importance of the transpiration stream. **2**

   (10)

In question 2, **ONE** mark is available for coherence and **ONE** mark is available for relevance.

2. Answer **either** A **or** B.

   A. Give an account of the mechanisms and importance of temperature regulation in endotherms. **(10)**

   OR

   B. Give an account of the effect of light on shoot growth and development, and on the timing of flowering in plants and breeding in animals. **(10)**

[END OF QUESTION PAPER]

SPACE FOR ANSWERS

SPACE FOR ANSWERS

SPACE FOR ANSWERS

SPACE FOR ANSWERS

ADDITIONAL GRAPH PAPER FOR QUESTION 2(*g*)

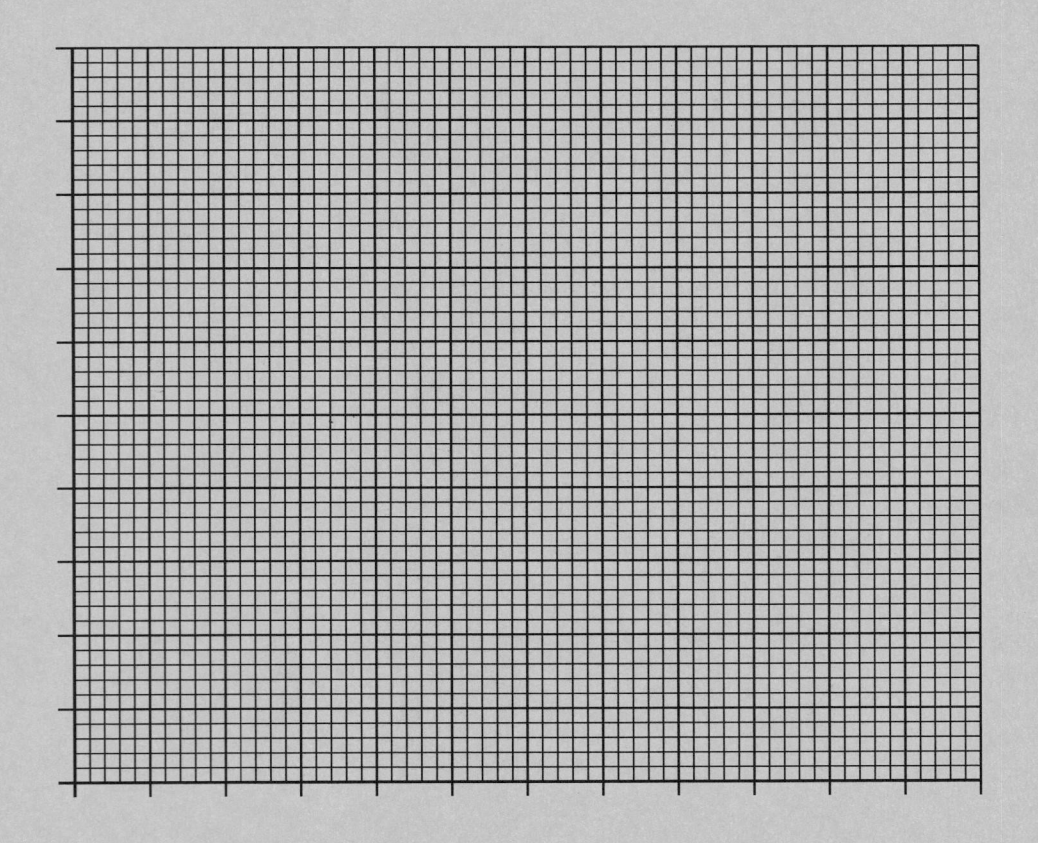